W9-ABG-635

ISSUES THAT CONCERN YOU

Gun Violence

Ronnie D. Lankford Jr., *Book Editor*

Christine Nasso, *Publisher*
Elizabeth Des Chenes, *Managing Editor*

GREENHAVEN PRESS
An imprint of Thomson Gale, a part of The Thomson Corporation

THOMSON
GALE
™

Detroit • New York • San Francisco • New Haven, Conn. • Waterville, Maine • London

Codman Sq. Branch Library
690 Washington Street
Dorchester, MA 02124-3511

JAN - - 2007

© 2007 Thomson Gale, a part of The Thomson Corporation.

Thomson and Star Logo are trademarks and Gale and Greenhaven Press are registered trademarks used herein under license.

For more information, contact
Greenhaven Press
27500 Drake Rd.
Farmington Hills, MI 48331-3535
Or you can visit our Internet site at http://www.gale.com

ALL RIGHTS RESERVED.
No part of this work covered by the copyright hereon may be reproduced or used in any form or by any means—graphic, electronic, or mechanical, including photocopying, recording, taping, Web distribution or information storage retrieval systems—without the written permission of the publisher.

Articles in Greenhaven Press anthologies are often edited for length to meet page requirements. In addition, original titles of these works are changed to clearly present the main thesis and to explicitly indicate the author's opinion. Every effort is made to ensure that Greenhaven Press accurately reflects the original intent of the authors.

Every effort has been made to trace the owners of copyrighted material.

LIBRARY OF CONGRESS CATALOGING-IN-PUBLICATION DATA

Gun violence / Ronnie D. Lankford Jr., book editor.
   p. cm. — (Issues That Concern You)
    Includes bibliographical references and index.
   ISBN-13: 978-0-7377-3241-2 (hardcover)
   ISBN-10: 0-7377-3241-5 (hardcover)
   1. Gun control—United States. 2. Violent crimes—United States. I. Lankford, Ronald D., 1962-
   HV7436G8758 2007
   363.330973—dc22
                                                        2006033098

Printed in the United States of America

CONTENTS

Newspaper reports of school shootings, sniper attacks, and assaults with a firearm by disgruntled employees have become common in the American press. Some sensational crimes capture national attention: For example, on April 20, 1999, Eric Harris and Dylan Klebold killed twelve students and a teacher and wounded twenty-eight others before committing suicide at Columbine High School in Colorado. On October 2, 2002, John Allen Muhammad and Lee Boyd Malvo, collectively referred to as the Beltway snipers, began a killing spree in the Washington, D.C. area that continued until their capture on October 22. On July 1, 2003, Jonathan Russell arrived at work at the Modine Manufacturing Company in Jefferson City, Missouri, and opened fire on his fellow employees, killing three and wounding five before killing himself. These and many similar crimes have become familiar scenarios in contemporary American society.

But a glance at headlines from around the world shows that gun violence is not a problem unique to America. On September 27, 2001, for example, disgruntled Swiss Friedrich Leibacher opened fire in his regional parliament chambers, killing fifteen Swiss officials and wounding fourteen more. In Erfurt, Germany, an April 2002 public school shooting spree left eighteen dead, including the nineteen-year-old gunman, and more recent school shootings have occurred in both France and Belgium. These incidents lead one to ask: How does gun violence in America compare with that of other countries?

One way to answer the question is by comparing firearm death rates, a figure that includes homicides, suicides, and accidents involving guns. A comparison of international firearm death rates, however, reveals two different stories. Considering all countries by the measure of firearm deaths alone, the United States has a lower firearm death rate than nonindustrialized countries such as Brazil and Argentina. But it is difficult to draw conclusions from these data because so many variables—living conditions, economic conditions—are very different in non-industrialized countries and industrialized countries.

Therefore, the significance of firearm death rates is clearer when the comparison is between the United States and other industrialized nations, which have similar types of economies and standards of living. When the U.S. firearm death rate is compared to that of industrialized countries such as Great Britain or Japan, a very different picture emerges. Indeed, the United States has the highest firearm death rate among all industrialized countries, accounting for an estimated thirty thousand American deaths per year. As the Violence Policy Center, an organization that works to reduce gun violence, has put it, "When compared to other industrialized nations, the United States stands alone in the number of its citizens felled by guns."

The difference between the United States and its industrialized counterparts is striking. In Western Europe, for instance, the annual firearm death rate is significantly lower than that of the United States. That region's lowest rate, .32 deaths per 100,000 people in Scotland, compares to 10.27 per 100,000 in the United States. In Japan, the annual firearm death rate per 100,000 people is .06—even lower than Scotland's. "In Japan, seventeen people were killed with guns in all of 1996," writes David Hemenway in *Private Guns, Public Health*. "More are killed in the United States on a slow afternoon."

Central to the issue of gun violence is the question, Why is the firearm death rate in the United States so much higher than in other industrialized nations? Critics often point to differences in firearm regulation and availability. There are approximately 200 million guns in the United States, a startling number in a nation of fewer than 300 million people. Indeed, it is estimated that a full 30 percent of Americans own at least one gun. "Guns are the 12th most common cause of death overall," notes Philip Cohen of the impact of guns on American society in the *New Scientist*, "and second only to road vehicles in deaths caused by injury."

In contrast, in Japan there are very few privately owned firearms, and an individual who wants to own a firearm must apply for a license and register the weapon. The same is true in England;

moreover, both Japan and England have banned handguns. Yet some experts dispute the idea that the mere presence of guns contributes to the difference in firearm death rates. For example, John R. Lott Jr. of the American Enterprise Institute points out that within the United States, the states with the highest gun ownership rates also have by far the lowest violent crime rates. Says Lott: "Guns surely make it easier to kill people, but guns also make it much easier for people to defend themselves."

There is heated debate over the possible causes of the difference in firearm death rates in the United States and in other countries, and scholars, law enforcement officials, sociologists, and

Police investigate a Manassas, Virginia, gas station where a man was shot by the D.C. snipers in 2002.

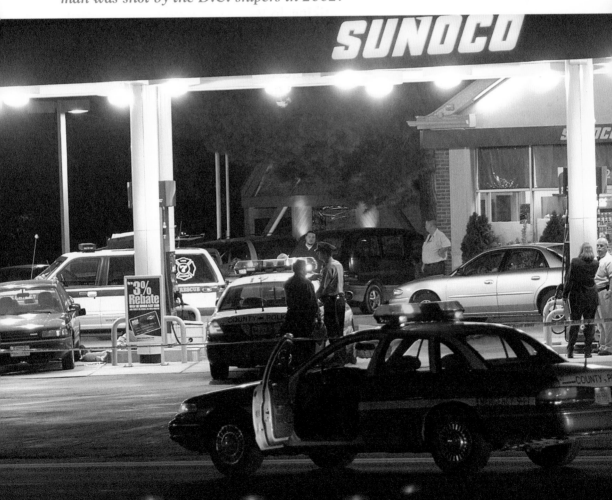

A gunsmith works on a rifle barrel in England, where the firearm death rate is much lower than that in the United States.

other authorities will continue to probe the issue as long as gun violence continues to threaten American lives. How America's gun violence rate compares to that of other countries is just one topic explored in *Issues That Concern You: Gun Violence*. In a variety of essays contributors explore topics such as whether gun control increases or decreases gun violence, how women are affected by gun violence, and other critical issues.

ONE

Gun Control Will Reduce Violence

Kevin Fagan

In the following viewpoint, Kevin Fagan argues that gun control can reduce violence. He discusses his personal experience with firearms, explaining the deadly role they have played in his life. While citizens may feel safer with a firearm for protection, he argues, the presence of firearms often leads to deadly violence—more than nine thousand people are murdered by handguns every year. Restricting the number of guns in America is the only way to end the violence. Fagan is a reporter for the *San Francisco Chronicle*.

My first real memory of a gun is from when I was 8, standing in a Nevada salt flat with my mother leaning over my right shoulder, folding my hand around the oh-so-smooth butt of a .22-caliber revolver. It was the gun she always kept under the car seat.

I squeezed off a shot at a rusty soda can 30 feet away, and the explosion in my ear and puff of sand alongside the can sent a shiver right to my toes.

"You'll get it, don't worry. You need to learn how to shoot this," my mother said, patting my head. "You never know how you might need it someday."

Kevin Fagan, "And That's the Trouble: The Gun Debate, Personalized," *San Francisco Chronicle*, January 8, 2006, p. 20. Copyright © 2006 San Francisco Chronicle. Republished with permission of San Francisco Chronicle, and Copyright Clearance Center.

She was right. I did learn how to shoot, and I did need a gun someday . . . several somedays. And I came to respect the way a gun could save my life.

I also came to hate guns for the ways they have just as easily, just as coldly, unthinkingly, devastated life around me and come close to ending my own life time and again.

And I've come to believe guns have no logical, meaningful place in the lives of most ordinary people.

caglecartoons.com/espanol

"City and Violence," cartoon by Alen Lauzan Falcon. Copyright © 2004 Alen Lauzan Falcon. All rights reserved. Reproduced by permission of Cagle Cartoons.

The Truth About Guns

There are plenty of Americans who have had the same relationship with this deadly little dealer of instant death. You could say the same thing about the country as a whole. It's a dysfunctional relationship, and there's not even a remotely easy way to fix it.

I'm not talking here about guns in the context of casual canplinking, or deer hunting, both of which are plenty of fun (Bambi lovers, chill) and don't threaten anything if done right. I'm talking about the stuff that makes America the Wild West barbarian outpost which people from other countries shake their heads about. I mean the real gun stuff that happens when you're staring life in the face, not being chauffeured to Congress past the rabble so you can blather Second Amendment platitudes and cash your NRA [National Rifle Association] lobby checks.

Top Five Crime Gun Dealers in America

Five stores – one in Indiana, one in Louisiana, one in California, one in North Carolina, and one in Wisconsin – sell the most guns that end up being used in crimes.

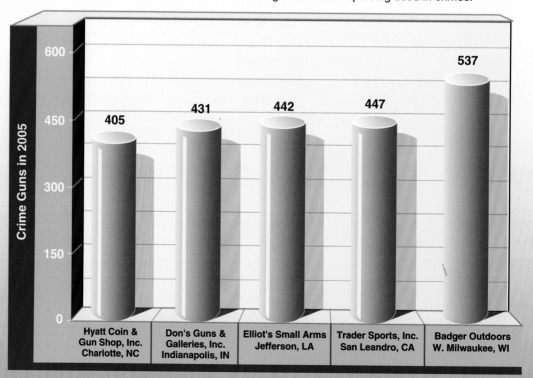

Source: Bureau of Alcohol, Tobacco, Firearms, and Explosives, May 2005.

Let me elaborate.

One relative of mine was blown away when he and his brother played stick-em-up in the family barn; they didn't know the shotgun was loaded. Another was nearly blasted in half when a robber shot him through his front door. A cousin lost use of her arm for years after being shot in the Marin County Courthouse shootout of 1970; the judge's head was blown off as he sat next to her.

Those were the things I experienced, but didn't see. Other times guns cut closer.

Guns Cause Needless Violence

In college in San Jose, I had to chase off attackers with a Luger 9mm semiautomatic when I lived alongside two warring gangs that promised to rub me out for telling the cops they shot holes in my windows and ripped off my car tires and gas. Years later, I had to replace that long-lost Luger with a .25-caliber semiautomatic when I was a young police reporter on a small-town newspaper and got a drug dealer mad at me.

I'd written a story about how this coke pusher kept squirming out of charges because the witnesses against him disappeared with each case. He told me to stop writing about him. When I gave him my Journalism 101 lecture about the First Amendment and wrote again, he stomped into my newspaper office.

"You're dead, . . . ," he said, jamming his face close to mine. His rapsheet already included a juvenile sentence for murder and two assault convictions with knives and a shotgun. The local police commander shook his head when I asked what he could do to protect me. "Better get a gun, son," he said.

My dad's .25 was under my pillow the next night, after I'd spent the afternoon blasting at targets. At 2 A.M. someone came slamming on my door, and I sat in the living room with the gun pointed straight ahead, screaming, "'Bring it on, . . . !" at the door. Whoever was outside screamed back, "You're dead!" I yelled back again; this went on awhile, and then he went away.

No doubt: I would have fired. Just as I might have in other situations over the years when gangsters I was trying to interview stuck pistols in my guts or to my head, or when my wife was robbed at gunpoint in Berkeley.

De-Escalate Confrontations by Removing Guns
And that's the trouble.

If none of us had had guns—most particularly, those handy little handguns—all these confrontations would have simply involved yelling, fists or perhaps knives.

In Great Britain, about 50 people die by handgun every year. In America? It's about 9,000. I've lived in both places, and let me tell you, your radar for—and encounters with—danger are so drastically reduced across the water that they are nonexistent by comparison.

Absolutely, if you're a law-abiding citizen and some predator is pointing a barrel at you, you want a barrel of your own to end the argument. But as plain as the blood on the floor every day in America, that's a perpetual tit-for-tat that will always be awful.

The only way to fix this hideously dysfunctional relationship we in this country have with guns is to treat it like you would any other: End it before you wind up murdered.

Nobody's saying this will be easy. The important things never are.

TWO

Gun Control Will Not Reduce Violence

Mark Alexander

> Mark Alexander is the executive editor and publisher of the *Federalist Patriot*, an online policy journal. In the following viewpoint, he argues that gun control advocates exploit tragedies like the Columbine school shooting to pass unreasonable gun control laws. Guns are not to blame for these tragedies, he argues: popular culture is. He blames gun violence on a lack of parental involvement in kids' lives, along with a lack of morals and ethics. Furthermore, actors often appear in movies that glorify violence which send the message to kids that violence is acceptable. Alexander concludes that if Americans want to see a reduction in violence they must improve aspects of their society that encourage it.

"The right of the citizens to keep and bear arms has justly been considered as the palladium of the liberties of a republic. . . "
—Justice Joseph Story

In the wake of another school shooting by another sociopathic teenager, Second Amendment opponents are again out in force attempting to convert the blood of innocents into political capital for gun confiscation.

Mark Alexander, "The 'Gun Problem,'" *Have Gun Will Vote*, April 5, 2005. www.havegunwill vote.com.

Among the first to demagogue the issue was Brady Campaign gun control advocate Michael Barnes, who condemned the "gun problem" and criticized Congress and President George W. Bush for letting the so-called "assault weapons" ban expire. Million Mom Marcher Kate Havelin howled, "We need to do more to make sure. . . our young people are safe from gun violence."

In an observation typical of the gun confiscation crowd's Leftmedia trucklings, *Washington Post* Deputy Editor Colbert King posed this loaded question: "What about the guns that take away the life?"

"Gun problem," "gun violence" and "guns that take away the life"? Like Barnes and Havelin, King insists that the problem is guns and that confiscating guns will solve the problem. But Barnes, Havelin and King, like most Leftists, display a chronic disconnect with reality. The "problem" in Red Lake, Minnesota (nine dead), is similar to that which visited Columbine High School in Littleton, Colorado (thirteen dead), back in 1999.

The Culture Problem

What was the problem? Leftists brace yourself: It was not a gun problem, but a culture problem. Amazingly, Barnes inadvertently touched on this problem, saying, "Our leaders are preaching about the culture of life. They should spend the same amount of energy taking steps to stop our nation's culture of death." Of course, Barnes and his ilk think the culture of death begins and ends with guns. Their silence on the real cultural problems is deafening.

Like the Columbine murderers, the 16-year-old Red Lake sociopath was obsessed with "Goth" culture. Similarly, he played violent video games and was fascinated with the ultra-Leftist Hitlerian Nazi anarchist movement. And, likewise, he asked some of his victims "Do you believe in God?" before gunning them down.

Of course, focusing on inanimate objects like guns is far easier than focusing on cultural problems, particularly since many of the problems in question are the result of Leftist doctrines—like parents (particularly fathers) who have abdicated the responsibility for raising responsible and moral children to government schools. The cultural consequences of renouncing that responsibility are exacerbated by the phony "Wall of Separation" arguments, which Leftjudicial activists have used to eliminate religious (read: "moral") training from those schools, and remove the Ten Commandments in principle and substance.

The best teachers in America are barely holding the high ground in classrooms where half the kids are under-parented (at best). The Left's response is to treat disorderly children and youth for ADD or (as was the case in Red Lake) with more powerful drugs like Prozac.

Not to be overlooked is yet another sacred cow of the Left—the "entertainment" industry's perverse glorification of murder, mayhem and drug use. Typical of Leftist hypocrisy, it is those Hollywonk "actors" making the biggest bucks on the bloodiest big screen splashes who are advocating for gun confiscation. Even allegedly "moderate" actors like Arnold Schwarzenegger, who, in his worst role yet as Governor of California recently signed a gun-ban, reached his position in life making films featuring wholesale slaughter and/or disembowelment of innocent folks.

Intentions

Founder John Adams wisely noted, "Facts are stubborn things; and whatever may be our wishes, our inclination, or the dictates of our passions, they cannot alter the state of facts and evidence." Indeed, the fact is, the Left's assertions about the "gun problem" simply don't hold up under scrutiny.

If the problem of criminal misuse of firearms was dependent on the availability of guns, research would demonstrate that the prevalence of firearms is directly related to violent gun crimes—that is, the more guns in an area, the more criminal gun use. However, any such relationship has been refuted by multiple and differing analyses. All studies inevitably lead to this conclusion: The crime problem is not about implements but intentions, and intent is inexorably defined by culture. Guns as implements are irrelevant to the criminal mindset that must perforce precede the decision to commit violence. To wit, despite Leftmedia folklore, the most violent attack on a school occurred on 18 May 1927 when Andrew Kehoe, a Bath, Michigan, school board member, murdered 45 people, including 38 elementary students—with a bomb.

Yale researcher John Lott addressed the relationship between gun possession and crime, and concluded his research with the title of his 1998 book, "*More Guns, Less Crime.*" Notably, Lott's research also determined this corollary to be fact: The countries that ban guns have the highest homicide rates. And why is this true? Intended victims are much easier to murder when their government has already disarmed them through gun control laws.

So, what about internal U.S. murder rates tracked against gun access over time? In 1900, the U.S. homicide rate was estimated at 1 per 100,000. In 2003, FBI statistics put the rate at 5.7 per 100,000. But during the 20th Century, gun availability was inversely related to these numbers; nearly anyone could buy and carry a gun in 1900, whereas there were 23,000 federal, state and local restrictions on firearms purchases by the end of the century.

Consider the comparable murder rates in the adjacent states of Massachusetts (very restrictive gun laws), versus Maine and New Hampshire (unrestrictive gun laws). Rates for crimes committed with guns are lower in Maine and New Hampshire than in Massachusetts. Furthermore, cities with the most restrictive gun laws, like Washington, D.C., and Atlanta, Georgia, have the highest murder rates in the nation.

Similarly, U.S. murder rates have trended downward in the last decade as more states have implemented "right to carry" laws, which make the criminal task of choosing unarmed victims more difficult. To paraphrase Thomas Sowell, "Most criminals aren't that stupid; they tend to go where the guns aren't."

Gun Control Around the World

The same correlations are in evidence around the world. Nations with the highest per-capita possession of firearms, such as Switzerland (where most households contain at least one "assault weapon" as part of their "well regulated militia") are among those

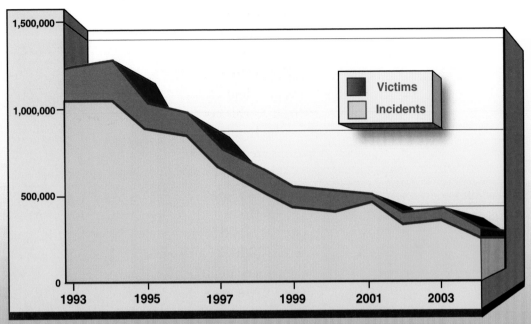

Nonfatal Firearm-Related Violent Crimes, 1993–2004

Victims

Incidents

The violent crimes included are rape and sexual assault, robbery, and aggravated assault.

Source: National Crime Victimization Survey (NCVS).

with the lowest murder rates. Conversely, nations like the UK, with the most restrictive gun laws, are now experiencing escalating crime rates.

The UK's gun restrictions, for example, did not stop a sociopath from slaughtering 16 kindergarteners and their teacher in Dunblane, Scotland, three years before Columbine. As a result of that shooting, all handguns were confiscated (similar to Sen. Diane Feinstein's proposal after Columbine). The result? By 2002, England and Wales had the highest incidence of "very serious" offences (18 crimes per 100 people) among the 17 developed Western nations. Second in line is Australia (16 per 100) where many classes of guns have also been confiscated. The incidence of "violent crime" is 3.6 per 100 in the UK, compared with 1.9 per 100 in the U.S.

A young boy approaches a memorial outside of the school in Dunblane, Scotland, where sixteen children were shot and killed in 1996.

Gun confiscation has never protected anyone. Gun restrictions have not protected citizens in Atlanta, Washington, D.C., New York or Boston, much less anyone in Columbine or Red Lake. Nor did such laws protect Jews from Hitler or Stalin or Chinese peasants from Mao, etc., ad infinitum.

In his *Commonplace Book*, Thomas Jefferson quotes Cesare Beccaria from his seminal work, *On Crimes and Punishment*: "Laws that forbid the carrying of arms . . . disarm only those who are neither inclined nor determined to commit crimes. . . . Such laws make things worse for the assaulted and better for the assailants; they serve rather to encourage than to prevent homicides, for an unarmed man may be attacked with greater confidence than an armed man." Again, no less true today than it has been throughout history.

Guns Are Not the Problem

The next time some Chardonnay-sipping Leftists pontificate about the "gun problem," remind them that far more Americans, particularly children, die as a result of alcohol abuse, than at the hands of criminals using guns. Would a five-day waiting period on the purchase of a good bottle of wine prevent those injuries and deaths?

As for the Marching Moms, it's worth noting that women are the fastest-growing demographic group of gun owners. And for good reason. It's now estimated that guns are used defensively more than 2.5 million times annually—four times more often than the estimated use of a gun in commission of a crime.

In short, culture trumps firearm access in determining murder rates, and if our murder rates are going to be further reduced, Americans of all political feathers would be well advised to take a sobering look at the cultural components which breed such violence, not the instruments used to commit violence.

THREE

The Gun Industry Should Be Held Responsible for Gun Violence

Allen Rostron

> In the following viewpoint, Allen Rostron argues that the Protection of Lawful Commerce in Arms Act (PLCAA) of 2005 unfairly grants gun manufacturers immunity from most lawsuits. He believes that gun manufactures should be held accountable when guns are sold irresponsibly. Making gun manufacturers and dealers liable for any crime committed with an illegally acquired gun is the only way to get the industry to keep guns away from those who shouldn't have them, he concludes. Allen Rostron is an associate Professor at the University of Missouri–Kansas City School of Law and a former staff attorney for the Brady Center to Prevent Gun Violence.

Americans have always cherished certain ideals about our justice system. You may win or you may lose, but you are entitled to have your day in court.

Last week [October 2005], President [George W.] Bush created a significant exception to that principle when he signed the "Protection of Lawful Commerce in Arms Act," a federal law that

Allen Rostron, "Dodging the Bullet: Tort Immunity for Gun Makers," *Jurist*, November 3, 2005. Reproduced by permission.

gives the gun industry a broad, nationwide immunity from legal responsibility for its actions. If the legislation survives constitutional challenges, gun makers and dealers will enjoy a level of protection from tort liability shared by no other industry.

The NRA [National Rifle Association], gun companies, and their allies have been pushing hard for this immunity law ever since Bush took office in 2001, and the only real surprise about

Some feel that the gun industry should be held accountable for gun violence.

its enactment is that it took so long. Supporters of the legislation insist that imposing liability on gun makers is an absurd notion akin to saying that manufacturers of pens should be blamed when people write bad checks.

Protection of Lawful Commerce in Arms Act

The statute generally bars claims brought against manufacturers, sellers, or trade associations concerning harm resulting from illegal misuse of a firearm or ammunition. In other words, if Beretta carelessly distributes a firearm in a way that makes it easy for a criminal to obtain it, Beretta will have no liability to the victims of murders, assaults, robberies, or other crimes committed with the gun.

The new law contains exceptions protecting several narrow categories of claims. For example, a person may be held liable for knowingly selling a gun in violation of federal or state law or neg-

"Gun Lobby (Silencer)," cartoon by Mike Keefe, *Denver Post* 2000. Copyright © 2002 Mike Keefe. All rights reserved. Reproduced by permission of Cagle Cartoons.

ligently entrusting a gun to someone the seller knows or reasonably should know is likely to use it in a harmful manner. While those exceptions will preserve some tort claims against retail gun dealers, they have little relevance to the liability of manufacturers who sell their products through distributors and dealers rather than directly to the public. None of the tort claims brought against gun manufacturers in recent years would fit within the exceptions.

The immunity legislation forced many of its proponents to take positions contrary to their usual ideological inclinations. Conservatives on Capitol Hill and in the White House supported the law despite the fact that it relies on a very broad view of Congress's authority under the Commerce Clause to impose nationwide regulations and to trump the public policy prerogatives of state governments.

The law's backers also emphasized that thirty-three states had already enacted statutes giving gun makers varying amounts of protection from tort liability. Rather than seeing that state-by-state decision-making as an illustration of federalism's virtues, the new law's supporters insisted that a single federal resolution of the issue had to be forced on every state for the sake of nationwide uniformity.

When Are Gun Manufacturers Liable?

During the debates over the bill, members of Congress repeatedly declared that firearm manufacturers should not be held liable every time a violent criminal misuses a gun. Public opinion polls indicate that the vast majority of Americans agree with that proposition. I spent several years helping to bring lawsuits against gun makers and I agree completely that a gun manufacturer should not be liable every time someone gets shot. The real issue, missed by those legislators and pollsters, is whether a gun manufacturer should be liable when it distributes or designs guns in unnecessarily and unreasonably dangerous ways and creates risks above and beyond those inherent in the sale of firearms.

Lee Malvo is brought into court to be identified by a witness during the trial of D.C. sniper suspect John Allen Muhammad in 2003.

The lawsuits brought in recent years have targeted what virtually anyone would regard as egregious negligence. For example, in the lawsuit arising from the sniper shootings by John Allen Muhammad and John Lee Malvo that terrorized the Washington D.C. area in the fall of 2002, a manufacturer and dealer agreed to pay more than $2.5 million to settle claims brought by victims of the shooting and their families. The dealer's store security was so inadequate that it enabled Malvo, a juvenile, to pick up a Bushmaster assault rifle and simply walk out the door without paying for it. Audits of inventory, conducted by law enforcement both before and after Malvo's theft, revealed hundreds of other firearms missing from the store. Despite being aware of the dealer's irresponsible behavior and appalling track record, the rifle manufacturer insisted that the dealer was a "good customer" through which it was happy to distribute its products.

In another case, a Massachusetts gun maker, Kahr Arms, did not conduct background checks on its employees, did not test them for drug use, and had no metal detectors, x-ray machines, security cameras, or even security guards to prevent employee theft from its factory. An employee with a criminal record and a long history of drug addiction took advantage of the absence of security measures, stealing guns from the factory and reselling them to criminals to support his drug habit. One of the guns wound up being used in a shooting outside a night club and killing an innocent bystander. Even some of the nation's most ardent gun rights activists have acknowledged that the new federal immunity legislation goes too far in exempting manufacturers from liability in this situation.

Lawsuits Reduce Illegal Access to Guns

Lawsuits have uncovered many other similarly disturbing stories, as well as striking revelations about attitudes within the gun industry. Robert Ricker worked for nearly twenty years as a lawyer and lobbyist for the NRA and the largest gun industry trade association. In a sworn statement obtained in litigation, he acknowledged that gun manufacturers' distribution systems encourage and reward illegal activity by corrupt dealers and distributors. When was the last time you heard anyone say something like that about the pen industry?

Ricker described how tort litigation might finally overcome the industry's resistance to reforms that would reduce illegal access to guns. "Leaders in the industry have long known that greater industry action to prevent illegal transactions is possible," Ricker stated, but "until faced with a serious threat of civil liability for past conduct, leaders in the industry have consistently resisted taking constructive voluntary action to prevent firearms from ending up in the illegal gun market and have sought to silence others within the industry who have advocated reform."

The immunity bestowed on the gun manufacturers and dealers by the new statute eliminates that valuable threat of civil liability. Congress and President Bush have given the industry the special immunity it desperately wanted, but innocent people will bear the consequences of this misguided effort to reduce the gun industry's incentives to conduct business in safe, reasonable, and responsible ways.

FOUR

The Gun Industry Should Not Be Held Responsible for Gun Violence

Ed Quillen

> In the following viewpoint, Ed Quillen argues that people should not be allowed to sue gun manufacturers and retailers for violence committed with guns. He rejects the idea that gun makers and sellers should be held accountable for acts committed with their products. Quillen believes that each individual is responsible for his or her own actions, and accuses gun control advocates of trying to undermine the right to own a gun. Ed Quillen is a columnist for the *Denver Post*, from which this viewpoint was taken.

If he has not done so already, President George W. Bush will soon sign a bill which passed the Senate [on] July [29, 2005] and the House last week [Oct. 17, 2005]. It shields gun makers and sellers from lawsuits that might arise from misuse of their weapons, and it could produce an honest discussion of guns in America.

Ed Quillen, "Shooting Straight on Guns," *Denver Post*, October 25, 2005, p. B7. Copyright © 2005 The Denver Post. Reproduced by permission of the author.

Not the Fault of the Seller and Maker

The new federal law does not protect gun makers from ordinary product-liability litigation. That is, if the industry still produced revolvers like one my father once owned but never used—one he described as "kill behind and maim in front" because the cylinder would not align properly with the barrel so that lead sprayed every which way when it was fired—then the maker could still be sued for making a defective product.

But if some thug acquires a firearm and commits murder and mayhem, then under the new law, the gun industry is immune to litigation from the victims. They can sue the shooter, but not the gun maker or seller, so long as they were obeying the law in the production and distribution of the weapon.

On the surface, this seems quite fair. We have a Second Amendment to the federal constitution, which guarantees the right of the people "to keep and bear arms." That right would be rather meaningless if gun and ammunition makers were put out of business by product liability lawsuits.

Do Not Use Litigation to Try to Ban Guns

If people want to agitate for repeal of the Second Amendment by electing senators and representatives and state legislators who will appropriately amend the federal constitution, that's their right. But it should be done as an open political process, not in a sneaky way through product-liability litigation.

Further, we don't hold knife makers liable in stabbings, or hammer makers liable in gruesome clubbings. I've followed many libel suits, and was hit by one in 1980 (it was dismissed before trial by the district court, but the plaintiff appealed the dismissals up the ladder clear to the U.S. Supreme Court), but never have I seen the company that manufactured the typesetting machinery or printing press named among the defendants.

Every year, land-management agencies like the Forest Service and the Bureau of Land Management cite hundreds of drivers for taking their vehicles off the designated routes and onto fragile tundra and wetlands. But they don't go after the makers of four-wheel-drive vehicles, even though that sort of anti-social destruction is often encouraged by their commercials.

We Are Responsible for Our Own Actions

We generally assume that tools and technology are morally neutral, and that we humans are responsible for how we use them. The same tool I use for the happy task of opening envelopes with checks in them could also be used to stab someone in the heart—it's what I do with it, not the tool itself, which matters.

But this doesn't fully hold all the time, at least before the U.S. Supreme Court. In its ruling on [a 2005 case], the court held that a technology company can be held responsible for illegal acts committed, not by the company, but by users of the software.

Some argue that people, not the gun industry, are responsible for their actions with firearms.

Gun enthusiasts practice target shooting at an indoor range.

At issue were computer programs which made file-sharing fast and simple. The court found that the software companies—Grokster and StreamCast Networks—encouraged the sharing of copyrighted materials, which of course had the movie and music studios up in arms and going to court to fight piracy.

But even in this case, the Supreme Court did not say that peer-to-peer filesharing software should be illegal because it could be used to violate copyright laws. Instead, it said Grokster and StreamCast were promoting their technologies for illegal purposes, and thus the companies were liable.

Guns Are Made to Kill People

With the new protections, the gun industry won't have to worry about that. It will be able to dispense with pretense in its marketing. We might actually see some truthful gun ads, perhaps one that quotes William Barclay "Bat" Masterson: "Always remember that a six-shooter is made to kill the other fellow with and for no other reason on earth."

Honesty in advertising—won't it be wonderful? And that might inspire the anti-gun crowd to go about its crusade honestly, pursuing a constitutional amendment, rather than back-door approaches through product-liability suits. And then there could be an honest discussion about guns in America.

FIVE

Gun Ownership Increases Violence Worldwide

Wendy Cukier and Victor W. Sidel

In the following viewpoint, Wendy Cukier and Victor W. Sidel lament that firearm violence has reached epidemic proportions throughout the world. Both the World Health Organization and the International Committee of the Red Cross, they note, have stated that firearms have a devastating impact on civilian populations. The authors correlate gun ownership and violent crime: For example, as people's access to firearms rises in industrialized countries, the crime rate increases. Besides the impact on individual lives, Cukier and Sidel argue, policing firearm violence is expensive, diverting funds from public programs and stretching resources at medical facilities. The global gun trade has fed the epidemic of violence, making the regulation of firearms difficult in the countries that need it most. The authors conclude that the availability of guns makes the world a more dangerous place, especially for women and children. Wendy Cukier is a professor of information technology management at Ryerson University in Toronto, and cofounder of the Coalition for Gun Control; Victor W. Sidel is a professor of social medicine at the Montefiore Medical Center and Albert Einstein College of Medicine, and a cofounder of the public policy advocacy organization Physicians for Social Responsibility.

Wendy Cukier and Victor W. Sidel, *The Global Gun Epidemic: From Saturday Night Specials to AK-47s*, Praeger, 2006. Copyright © 2006 by Wendy Cukier and Victor W. Sidel. All rights reserved. Reproduced by permission of Greenwood Publishing Group, Inc., Westport, CT.

Firearms have been recognized as a public health problem in the United States for many years, yet attention to the issue on a global basis is relatively recent. It was not until 1996 that the World Health Organization labeled violence a pandemic. This was the same year that the International Committee of the Red Cross went on record, stating simply, "Weapons are bad for people's health," and, "health professionals have been slow to recognize that the effects of weapons are, by design, a health issue, and moreover constitute a global epidemic mostly affecting civilians." . . .

The Impact of Firearms

It is not surprising that the terms *epidemic* and *pandemic* are now being used in association with firearms. A look at the impact of firearms on human lives in terms of homicide, suicide, accidental death and injury illustrates the magnitude of the public health

"Gun World," cartoon by Alen Lauzan Falcon. Caglecartoons.com/espanol, September 22, 2003. Copyright © 2003 Alen Lauzan Falcon. All rights reserved. Reproduced by permission of Cagle Cartoons, Inc.

challenges posed by guns. Globally, approximately 200,000 people are estimated to have been killed annually in homicides, suicides and accidents with firearms, with thousands more killed in military conflicts. Although the exact number of small arms casualties in military conflicts is a matter of debate, there is no doubt that small arms are the weapons of choice in armed conflicts today and that the secondary impacts of these conflicts are immense. A large percentage of casualties are civilians, conservatively estimated by the International Committee of the Red Cross at more than 35 percent. In Iraq, for example, civilian casualties actually outnumber combatant deaths. While there has been intense focus on the deaths from small arms in the context of conflict, there are more deaths annually from firearms in the hands of civilians in countries not engaged in conflict. To put it bluntly: From a public health perspective, a dead child is a dead child, whether it is a child soldier in Uganda, a crime victim in Soweto or a student in Columbine High School in the United States. There is evidence that the threat to children from firearms is as great in some countries considered to be at peace as it is in conflict zones.

Fatality rates for suicides attempted with firearms tend to be much higher than those for attempted homicide; consequently, the rate of injury associated with suicide attempts is much lower. Of course, the impact of firearms is not restricted to fatalities. For every death caused by a firearm there are additional injuries requiring hospitalization. Studies in Brazil and South Africa, for example, report almost ten times more firearm injuries than fatalities, while in countries such as Finland and Canada, the reported mortality and injury rates are roughly equivalent. This difference may be related to the context in which the death and injury occur. Research shows that in Brazil and South Africa, the person firing the weapon is most likely attempting a homicide, while in Canada and Finland, the person is probably attempting suicide.

Women, Children, and Poor Are Victims

Some segments of the population are particularly hard hit, in both industrialized and developing countries. Women are seldom users of firearms but are often victims, both in the context of war and in domestic violence. A recent comparative study showed that guns figure prominently in the cycle of violence against women and children in Canada, Australia and South Africa. The patterns of weapons use in domestic violence are also remarkably consistent across cultures. In many industrialized countries, firearms are a leading cause of mortality among children and youth, with these groups representing a large percentage of the victims of conflict, both as combatants and as casualties. Furthermore, a number of studies have revealed that the poor are more likely to be victims of violence....

Costs to Mental and Physical Health

Violence and the prevalence of weapons also create psychological stress that fuels other health problems and creates insecurity. Arms-infested environments yield observable symptoms of post-traumatic stress disorder, such as overwhelming anxiety and a lack of motivation. Other secondary effects include problems related

Guns and Domestic Violence

Both male and female victims of domestic violence are most often killed with guns, according to the Bureau of Justice Statistics.

Relationship of victim to offender	Gun	Knife	Blunt Object	Force	Other Weapon
Husband	69%	26%	2%	1%	2%
Ex-husband	87%	9%	1%	0%	2%
Wife	68%	14%	5%	10%	4%
Ex-wife	77%	12%	2%	6%	3%
Boyfriend	46%	45%	3%	3%	3%
Girlfriend	56%	20%	5%	14%	5%

Homicides by relationship and weapon type, 1990-2004

Source: Bureau of Justice Statistics, "Homicide Trends in the U.S.," 2006.

Some studies indicate that the risk of dying from a gunshot wound is greater if a gun is kept in the home.

to a country's blood supply. Not only are blood availability and facilities for transfusion key issues in developing countries, but emergency responses to large-scale violence often do not accommodate careful testing for HIV and result in additional public health problems.

Violence has been identified as a major impediment to the provision of basic health care. Violence also diverts resources from other health and social services. In South Africa, scarce hospital resources are diverted from patients suffering from disease to deal with victims of gun violence. Even more troubling, health care personnel are themselves increasingly the target of violence because they attempt to save the lives of people who are the targets of violence. Furthermore, many injured victims die during transport rather than at treatment facilities, as the medical transportation infrastructure cannot carry the burden created by increased arms proliferation.

More Guns Equal More Deaths

The public health approach to injury prevention is multilayered and comprehensive and addresses the root causes of firearm death and injury at the individual and community levels. It also focuses our attention on the instrument of violence—the firearm—and the relationship between the availability of firearms and their misuse, particularly in industrialized nations. The link between accessibility of guns and levels of violence has been demonstrated in a number of contexts. Research does show, however, that high rates of gun ownership are generally related to high levels of arms-related violence in "conflict zones" as well as in countries that are "at peace."

Studies comparing homes where firearms are present to those where they are not have concluded that the risk of death is substantially higher if firearms are in the home. This is not to say that the presence of firearms in a home is the only contributing factor to violence. Certainly more research could illuminate the interactions of the range of factors shaping the demand for firearms, at the societal level and at the individual level, including criminal activity, drug use and parental factors.

Nevertheless, a growing body of literature reveals a relationship between access to firearms, and firearm death rates and rates of firearm crime in industrialized countries. . . . International comparisons show that among industrialized nations, the United States has by far the highest rates of firearm ownership as well as firearm death and injury. In contrast, rates of other violence in the United States, including murders committed without firearms, are comparable to rates found in other countries. This underpins the notion that reducing access to firearms through regulation could lead to a reduction in the lethality of conflicts, assaults, suicide attempts and accidents.

The Global Gun Trade

While there is a general consensus that firearms are dangerous and need to be regulated, there is no international consensus regarding what would constitute an appropriate domestic or global approach to regulation. To understand the challenges of regulating firearms, it is first necessary to understand the global gun trade, including the production of firearms for state and commercial uses. The international market for firearms is large and complex in terms of both the markets served and the players in the distribution chain, from production through use. Almost 100 countries are engaged in some aspect of firearm manufacture, although much of the production is concentrated in a few countries, including the five permanent members of the UN Security Council—the United States, Russia, China, the United Kingdom and France—plus a number of other European, Asian and Latin American countries. In many cases, the production of firearms is state controlled. Firearms manufacturers fall into two general categories: Those whose production is state controlled and tied very closely to defense industries, and those who focus on "consumer markets." The latter group is extremely diverse in terms of scale of operations and range of product offerings.

The global trade in firearms is not always transparent. It is well documented that legal firearms are diverted to illegal markets that fuel crime as well as political conflicts worldwide. Virtually every "illegal" small arm began as a legal one. An analysis of more than 200 reported incidents of illicit trafficking suggests that misuse and diversion occur through a variety of mechanisms that generally fall into three broad categories: (1) legally held firearms that are misused by their lawful owner (whether states, organizations or individuals); (2) legal firearms that are "diverted" into the "gray" market (sold by legal owners to unauthorized individuals, illegally sold, stolen or diverted through other means) and (3) illegally manufactured and distributed firearms (although these account for only a small fraction of the illicit gun trade).

There are more firearms in the possession of civilians worldwide than are held by governments and police, and diversion of these firearms, particularly in the United States, fuels illicit firearm markets and deaths worldwide. In many parts of the world, firearms diverted from legal markets in one country into illegal markets in another are a significant problem. Many nations in southern Africa, for example, have strict domestic controls on firearms and correspondingly lower crime rates compared to those in South Africa, where gun controls are far less strict. As a result, countries near South Africa, such as Lesotho and Botswana, must contend with a high rate of gun smuggling across their borders. In North America, U.S. guns are exported to the gray markets of neighboring countries Canada and Mexico. In Mexico, U.S. guns account for 80 percent of illegal firearms. In Canada about 50 percent of illegal handguns used in crime come from the United States. Proximity to a country with less stringent gun controls is not a prerequisite for "importing" guns. Consider, for example, that many of the firearms possessed by the Irish Republican Army (IRA) originated in the United States, and that guns in Japan come primarily from the United States, China and South Africa.

Gun Culture and the Demand for Firearms

In the United States there are almost as many guns as people—roughly 220 million, almost one-third of all the guns in the world. In the United States people own guns for a variety of reasons—hunting, target shooting, collecting and self-protection. The rates of firearm ownership in the United States are not seen elsewhere in the world. Most industrialized countries have much lower rates of gun ownership, and few allow civilians to carry guns for the purposes of protection. Firearm ownership rates range from less than 1 percent of households in countries such as England, Wales, Germany and Japan to about 20 percent in countries such as Canada, Austria and France and closer to 40 percent in countries such as Finland and Switzerland. But only a small percentage of firearms in these countries are handguns. The purposes for owning firearms vary considerably—some countries, such as Canada, Austria, and the United States, have extensive recreational hunting. Others, such as Kenya, use firearms to protect herds from predators. Many permit sporting uses of firearms for target shooting and collecting. In many contexts firearms are possessed, legally or illegally, as a means of promoting a sense of security in the face of crime or political instability. . . .

Regardless of the differences among cultures, one factor is constant—firearm possession is a predominantly male activity. Men dominate armies and police forces, and the vast proportion of hunters and target shooters worldwide is male. The link between masculinity and firearms permeates many cultures, both industrialized and developing. A range of cultural carriers, from traditional practices such as songs through electronic media such as video games and movies, reinforce these links and promote demand. Again, firearms sellers exploit many of these beliefs and values in their efforts to sell more guns.

There is also an interesting and complex dynamic between the supply of and the demand for firearms. Increased weapon availability has been shown to fuel a "culture of violence." More weapons tend to promote armed violence, which in turn promotes fear, which drives demand. The militarization of culture in South Africa illustrates this point. A number of studies have shown links between that country's culture of violence and civilian attitudes to firearms. Laws that control firearms both reflect and shape values, particularly the "culture of violence," in the same way legislation has been observed to have long-term effects on other

Civil rights activist Martin Luther King Jr. believed that lack of gun control laws increases gun violence.

behaviors. The concept that what a society tolerates, and what it legislates, shapes its behaviors and attitudes was eloquently voiced by Martin Luther King, Jr., more than forty years ago: "By our readiness to allow arms to be purchased at will and fired at whim; by allowing our movies and television screens to teach our children that the hero is one who masters the art of shooting and the technique of killing . . . we have created an atmosphere in which violence and hatred have become popular past-times." Consequently, it is not surprising that countries and regions with the highest levels of firearm violence and ownership are less able to address them than countries with low rates of firearm violence and ownership. Stricter controls on firearms both reflect and shape values, which is perhaps why countries with relatively low rates of gun ownership and crime are more able to move quickly to strengthen laws when tragedy strikes. The terrible irony is that countries with the highest rates of gun death and ownership are also the least able to effect change.

SIX

Gun Control Increases Violence Worldwide

John R. Lott Jr.

In the following viewpoint, John R. Lott Jr. argues that gun control does not curb violence, but actually contributes to it. He notes that although Australia, England, and other countries have strengthened gun control laws in recent years, crime rates there continue to grow because criminals are attracted to "safe zones," areas where gun control is most strict. Criminals flock there because they know they will not meet with armed resistance, Lott explains. Furthermore, the restriction of guns drives them to be sold on the black market, which makes the trade of weapons unregulatable by officials. While the United Nations has suggested stricter gun control measures as a means for reducing crime, Lott concludes that such measures fail to address the true causes of global violence. John R. Lott Jr. is a resident scholar at the conservative think tank American Enterprise Institute, and the author of More Guns, Less Crime: Understanding Crime and Gun Control.

Gun control advocates in the U.S. often point to Europe's strict gun laws as the example for the U.S. to follow. Yet, the three very worst public shootings during 2001 and the first half of 2002 all occurred in Europe. Around the world, from Australia to

John R. Lott Jr., *The Bias Against Guns: Why Almost Everything You've Heard About Gun Control Is Wrong.* Washington, DC: Regnery, 2003, pp. 72–78.

England, countries that have recently strengthened gun control laws have seen violent crime soar. Ironically, the gun laws are passed because politicians promise they will reduce these types of crime.

Shootings in Europe

Sixteen people were killed during an April 2002 public school shooting in Germany. The United States seems peaceful by comparison: Though the U.S. has almost five times as many students as Germany, thirty-two students and four teachers were killed from all types of gun death at elementary and secondary schools over almost five school years (August 1997 to June 2002).

Recent public school shootings have also occurred in France and Belgium, but shootings have not been limited to schools. The other two worst public shootings were the killing of fourteen regional legislators in Zug, a Swiss canton (September 2001), and the massacre of eight city council members in a Paris suburb (March 2002). . . .

"Safe Zones" and Black Markets

All three European killing sprees share one thing in common: They took place in so-called gun-free "safe zones." That criminals are attracted to gun-free zones is hardly surprising. Guns surely make it easier to kill people, but guns also make it much easier for people to defend themselves. As with many other gun laws, it is law-abiding citizens, not would-be criminals, who obey gun-free zones. Hence, "gun free" zones turn the law-abiding into sitting ducks.

In two of the European cases, the killers also managed to evade extensive laws on gun ownership. The killer of eight city council members in Paris was a psychiatric patient and did not have the required gun license. The killer of fourteen people in the canton parliament in Zug also had a history of mental illness. He falsified records to obtain a license for a military rifle.

After a long flirtation with gun free "safe zones," many Americans have learned their lesson the hard way. The U.S. has seen a gradual but significant change from 1985, when just eight states had right-to-carry laws. Today the number is thirty-three. And . . . deaths and injuries from multiple victim public shootings fell on average by 78 percent in states that passed such laws. The drop in the number of attacks—while not as large as the deaths and injuries resulting from those attacks—was still substantial. . . .

Violent crime is becoming a major problem in Europe. While many factors, such as law enforcement, drug gangs, and immigration affect crime, the lofty promises of gun controllers can no longer be taken seriously.

Police and children gather in front of a school in Erfurt, Germany, where a student shot and killed sixteen people in 2002.

Indeed, countries such as the United Kingdom and Australia have seen violent crime soar after the passage of strict gun prohibitions and even penalties for defensive gun use. Yet, both the U.K. and Australia have ideal conditions for gun control to work, as both countries are surrounded by water, making gun smuggling relatively difficult.

Of course, advocates of gun control look for ways to get around the new evidence. Publications such as the *New York Times* and the *Los Angeles Times* blame Europe's increasing crime problems on a seemingly unstoppable black market that "has undercut . . . strict gun-control laws." [Edmund L. Andrews]

Assume the black market is to blame for gun control's failure in these countries. Wouldn't smuggling be the natural consequence of these gun control laws? In the U.K. "gang and drug activity have propelled an influx of guns," [Sebastian Rotella] but it is not obvious why governments expect to be any more successful controlling the black market in guns than they have been in controlling the black market in drugs. It is hardly surprising that drug gangs will smuggle in guns along with their drugs if only to help them protect their illegal drug markets.

Gun Control Equals More Crime

Another inconvenient fact frequently ignored by gun control advocates is that many countries with very high homicide rates have either complete or virtually complete gun bans. Major countries such as Russia and Brazil have homicide rates several times that of the U.S. After decades of severe restrictions on gun ownership, Brazil temporarily tried to ban guns, but its supreme court eventually threw out the law. Other countries such as Colombia and Venezuela have even much higher homicide rates, but there are other obvious explanations (such as the drug trade).

The 2002 shooting in Germany was followed by the passage of even stricter gun laws, but increased crime in Europe is causing new center-right governments to rethink their reflexive support for more anti-gun laws. At the same time Germany was moving against guns, Italian defense minister Antonio Martino suggested that Italy model its laws after the U.S. Constitution's Second Amendment, which protects the right of citizens to bear arms.

The growing fears of crime may have been responsible for Jean-Marie Le Pen's upset second place showing in France's presidential elections in 2002. As a fifty-eight-year-old mother of two in France said: "My son was last week mugged—just for a cigarette! I've never done this before and you may not like to hear it, but I'm voting for Le Pen."

Many French politicians complained during their 2002 presidential election that the shooting in Paris meant "It's getting like in America, and we don't want to see that here." Americans may draw a different lesson from the evidence and hope that they don't become more like the Europeans.

The United Nations and Gun Control

The 2001 United Nations conference on small arms, which ended in controversy, had an admirable enough goal: to save lives. Some conference attendees claimed that guns used in armed conflicts cause 300,000 deaths worldwide every year. The international community's proposed solution? Prevent rebels from getting guns by requiring that "member states complete a registry of all small arms within their borders" and by "limiting the sale of such weapons only to governments."

This may be an understandable solution from governments that don't trust their citizens. But it also dangerously disregards their citizens' safety and freedom. For that reason, the [President George W.] Bush administration should be thanked, not scolded as it was by many, for effectively squelching the accord. Why? First, and most obviously, because not all insurgencies are bad. It is hardly surprising that infamous regimes such as those in Syria, Cuba, Rwanda, Vietnam, Zimbabwe, and Sierra Leone support these antigun provisions. Banning guns for rebels in totalitarian countries—because guns cause killings—is like arguing that wars are never justified.

Italian defense minister Antonio Martino has suggested that Italy model its gun laws after those in the United States.

In hindsight, would the international community really have preferred that Hitler's takeover of Europe go unresisted? Should the French or Norwegian resistance movements simply have given up? Surely this might have minimized war casualities.

Many countries today already totally ban private gun ownership, with Rwanda and Sierra Leone as two notable examples. With more than a million people hacked to death with knives and cleavers over the last seven years, were the citizens of

In an effort to decrease gun violence, the United Nations proposed limiting the sale of firearms to nations' governments.

Rwanda and Sierra Leone better off without guns to defend themselves?

What about the massacres of civilians in Bosnia? If Bosnians had possessed guns, would the massacres have taken place? And what about the Jews in the Warsaw ghetto during World War II? Would it not have been better if they had had more guns to defend themselves? With all the well-deserved publicity for the movie

Schindler's List, the movie left out how Schindler, an avid gun collector, stockpiled guns and hand grenades in case the Jews he was protecting needed to defend themselves. More recently, the proposed rules would have prevented the American government from assisting the Afghanis in their fight against the Soviet Union. When the Taliban took over during the mid-1990s, one of their first actions was to disarm the citizens. While people apparently complied without much resistance at the time, with hindsight it is not so obvious that this was really in their best interest.

The Crime–Gun Control Connection

There is a second important reason mentioned earlier for allowing citizens to keep small arms: Even in free countries, with little risk of a totalitarian regime, gun bans all but invariably result in higher crime. In the U.S., the states with the highest gun ownership rates also have by far the lowest violent crime rates. And similarly, over time, states with the largest increases in gun ownership have experienced the biggest drops in violent crime.

[Professor of economics] Jeff Miron at Boston University recently examined homicide rates across forty-four countries and found that the countries with the strictest gun control laws also had the highest homicide rates, though the higher rate was only statistically significant in half of his estimates. Miron does an excellent job accounting for different factors not previously accounted for in cross-country comparisons, and he uses data for a large set of countries (rather than subjectively selecting a half-dozen or a dozen as is normally done).

One particularly dramatic comparison was recently provided by [Professor] William Pridemore on the historical homicide rates in the U.S. and the former USSR. Using the actual homicide rate data for the Soviet Union and not the data that had been released for propaganda purposes, Pridemore shows that the USSR's homicide rate "has been comparable to or higher than the U.S. rate for at least the past 35 years." Indeed, during the entire decade from 1976 to 1985, the USSR's homicide rate was between 21 and 41 percent higher than that of the United States. By 1989, two years before the collapse of the Soviet Union, their homicide rate rose 48 percent above ours. Neither the ban on private ownership of guns nor the ruthless totalitarian-communist system that enforced this ban was able to produce a low homicide rate.

"Time-series" evidence that examines how crime rates change in only one particular area over time also provides some interesting relationships. In 1996, Britain banned handguns. Prior to that time, over 54,000 Britons owned handguns. The ban was so tight that even shooters training for the Olympics were forced to trav-

Gun Ownership Around the World

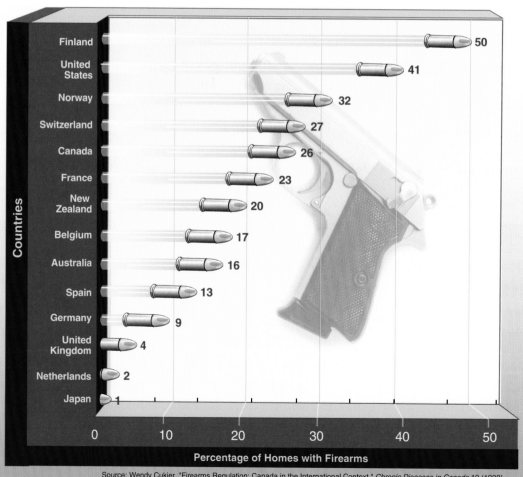

Source: Wendy Cukier, "Firearms Regulation: Canada in the International Context," *Chronic Diseases in Canada* 19 (1998).

el to Switzerland or other countries to practice. Four years have elapsed since the ban was introduced, and gun crimes have risen by an astounding 40 percent. The United Kingdom now leads the United States by an almost two-to-one margin in violent crime. Although murder and rape rates are still higher in the United States, the difference has been shrinking. A recent Associated Press Report notes "Dave Rogers, vice chairman of the [London] Metropolitan Police Federation, said the ban made little difference to the number of guns in the hands of criminals. . . . The underground supply of guns does not seem to have dried up at all."

Australia also passed severe gun restrictions in 1996, banning most guns and making it a crime to use a gun defensively. In the next four years, armed robberies there rose by 51 percent, unarmed robberies by 37 percent, assaults by 24 percent, and kidnappings by 43 percent. While murders fell by 3 percent, manslaughter rose by 16 percent. In Sydney, handgun crime rose by an incredible 440 percent from 1995 to 2001. Again, both Britain and Australia are "ideal" places for gun control as they are surrounded by water, making gun smuggling relatively difficult. The bottom line, though, is that these gun laws clearly did not deliver the promised reductions in crime.

SEVEN

Handgun Ownership Empowers Women

Rachel Jurado

> In the following viewpoint, Rachel Jurado argues that women need guns to protect themselves. She claims that women have been able to prevent crimes against themselves by carrying handguns and using them in self-defense. In addition to endangering women, gun control also endangers minorities who live in inner cities, Jurado states, by limiting the self-protection they need in such hazardous neighborhoods. Although some feminists have argued for stricter gun control, Jurado concludes that guns can empower women and other vulnerable people by giving them the means to protect themselves against attackers. Rachel Jurado is an assistant editor for the *American Interest* and a writer for *American Enterprise*.

In the middle of a long drive through rural Texas in the early 1960s, Evelyn Logan pulled over at a rest stop at 5:30 A.M. to take a break. As she emerged from the public bathroom, a man ambushed her, grabbed her by the hair, and dragged her toward the nearby woods. All Evelyn could do at first was scream for help—as she had five years earlier when she was raped in an airport parking garage.

Rachel Jurado, "Gun Control Victims: Women Receive Little Encouragement for Self-Defense from Mainstream Feminists," *American Enterprise*, January/February 2004, pp. 44–45. Copyright 2004 American Enterprise Institute for Public Policy Research. Reproduced with permission of *The American Enterprise*, a national magazine of politics, business, and culture (taemag.com).

But then she reached into her purse for the .22 handgun she kept there. She shot at the ground in front of her. The shock of the explosion allowed her to free herself from her attacker's grasp and take control of the situation. She forced him to lie prostrate on the ground next to the main road and then waited for someone to stop and help. Eventually, some policemen, who were patrolling the area for a serial rapist, pulled into the rest stop and arrested their man.

These traumatic events led Evelyn to her life's work: instructing women on the defensive use of firearms, as well as other methods of self-defense. "I am a rape survivor, and a rape-attempt survivor," she tells students. "The difference is, the second time I had a gun." Logan also serves as coordinator of the New Hampshire branch of the Second Amendment Sisters, a group of women opposed to gun control laws.

The Dangers of Gun Control

Although proponents claim that gun control laws help everyone, they may actually result in increased exposure to crime and violence for the most vulnerable members of society. The very first nationwide gun control efforts began in Nazi Nazi Germany and preceded Adolf Hitler's incapacitation and eventual murder of millions of citizens deemed "undesirable."

The Nazis started with benign anti-gun laws aimed at fighting gang violence. Then the controls were extended. The day after the infamous [1938] Kristallnacht rampages, Berlin's police president Wolf Heinrich von Helldorf boasted that the Jewish population of Berlin had been completely disarmed in the weeks preceding the event. All told, the police confiscated 1,702 guns, 20,000 rounds of ammunition, and 2,569 other small weapons from Jews. The next day, von Helldorf warned that any Jews with unlicensed weapons would face "the severest punishment."

An armed Jewish population could have done much more to defend itself against future horrors. During the Warsaw Ghetto uprising [of 1943], a small group of freedom fighters using improvised weapons and a few smuggled guns managed to put up stiff resistance for nearly a month. With a greater arsenal, Europe's Jews might have been able to fight a full-fledged guerilla war against the Nazis.

This narrative is, of course, very familiar to Second Amendment advocates, who often cite it as the clearest case of what can happen when a citizenry allows itself to be disarmed by its government. Much closer to home, however, is a cautionary tale from America's own history: the post-Civil War South. During Reconstruction, Negro militias were established in several states, but during the Jim Crow era that followed, state lawmakers used our country's first gun control laws and registration requirements to disarm blacks physically and, by extension, politically.

Today's gun control movement sidesteps any acknowledgement of the political repercussions of current and past gun control policies. Senator Dianne Feinstein states simply that, "Banning guns addresses a fundamental right of Americans to feel safe." Unfortunately this bit of high-minded rhetoric masks an important shift of power from citizens to government authorities. Moreover, such a policy would victimize individuals who, like Evelyn Logan, would be left with no means to defend themselves.

Gun Control's Effect on the Marginalized

Gun control policies also hit urban Americans hard, especially the poor and marginalized. Crime goes unchecked in many inner cities most of all because law-abiding residents are unable to protect themselves. Gun bans, licensing fees, legalese on application forms, and so forth make it impossible for many city dwellers to own a gun for self-defense. Take Ronald Dixon.

Unlike many of the most vocal gun control advocates, Dixon did not have bodyguards, high-priced lawyers, or celebrity status to protect him, so he bought a gun in Florida from a licensed firearms dealer. When he moved to Brooklyn in 2002, Dixon was required to obtain a gun license. Because of the legal hoopla involved, he paid a company $550 to process the paperwork for him.

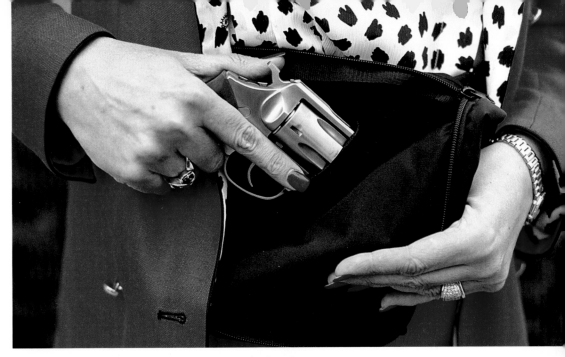

Some women choose to own guns to feel safer.

Soon after, on the morning of December 14, Dixon watched from his bedroom as a complete stranger walked blithely past his door and down the hall. He grabbed his gun and followed the man, only to find him in his son's room rifling through the drawers. Dixon warned the man to leave; the burglar attacked, and Dixon was forced to shoot him. Things only became more complicated after the shooting. The registration process for the gun was not yet complete when the incident occurred, and so Brooklyn District Attorney Charles Hynes (who once let a woman who scalded her daughter to death get off without being charged) slapped Dixon with a misdemeanor for illegal gun possession and proposed a four-week jail sentence. Eventually Hynes reduced the charge to disorderly conduct, and in June 2003, Dixon spent a day in the same jail as his burglar, Ivan Thompson.

People Suffer When Unable to Protect Themselves

Though liberal interest groups like the NAACP [National Association for the Advancement of Colored People], the

Women practice target shooting at an outdoor range. Organizations such as the Second Amendment Sisters educate women on gun use.

National Organization for Women, the Gay and Lesbian Alliance Against Discrimination, and the Anti-Defamation League have strong anti-gun platforms, the historical reality is that African Americans, women, homosexuals, and Jews have suffered physically and politically in the past because of their inability to protect themselves. Recognizing this, grassroots groups like the Second Amendment Sisters, Jews for the Preservation of Firearms Ownership, and the Pink Pistols have sprung up to promote and protect the rights of ownership and the safe use of firearms for members of historically oppressed groups.

Kenneth Blanchard, a black preacher and Second Amendment activist, says that the NAACP "sold us out" in order to curry political favor with other activist groups on the left, for whom gun control is a kind of gospel. Too many blacks have let their Second Amendment rights slip away, following instead a "mentality that prefers comfort to freedom"—that prefers passive reliance on others to ensure one's own safety. Blanchard has worked since 1991 to promote gun ownership and education among blacks. He founded a shooting club for blacks named after the Buffalo soldiers of the U.S. Army: the Tenth Cavalry Gun Club.

The first chapter of the Pink Pistols, a gay pro-gun group, was formed in 1993. Since then 37 chapters have formed in 28 states. The group gained notoriety in 1998 when one of its Massachusetts chapters ardently criticized gay State Senator Cheryl Jacques (D) for sponsoring a strict anti-gun bill that eventually passed in the statehouse. The bill amended state gun licensing laws such that the power to decide which citizens could obtain licenses lay solely in the hands of district police chiefs. The group challenged Jacques to view the bill as one that would negatively affect marginalized groups. Under the measure, Pink Pistols spokesman David Rostcheck complained, "[a] police chief can deny a license to a legally qualified person based on their gender, their housing, their sexual orientation—absolutely anything they want."

A Woman's Right to Feel Safe

Second Amendment groups have recognized the growing interest of women in gun ownership and have begun to cater to their specific needs with women's training classes, hunting trips, and shooting sports competitions. Most female gun owners want guns for self-defense, however. A number of organizations were formed in response to the hysterics of the Million Mom March in 2000. The Liberty Belles, Armed Females of America, and Women Against Gun Control have joined the Second Amendment Sisters in a coalition that seeks to educate women about the usefulness of guns as a means of self-defense, while encouraging women to become skilled enough with handguns so they can qualify for concealed-carry permits.

Women receive little encouragement for self-defense from mainstream feminists. When asked about the growing interest of women in the defensive use of firearms, Betty Friedan, the grandmother of modern feminism, called it "a horrifying, obscene perversion of feminism." On the religious Left, the Reverend Allen Brockway of the United Methodist Church has written, "Rather than shooting rapists, it is women's Christian duty to submit to rape." More and more women are choosing to ignore such counsel, though, and instead are acquiring the means to protect themselves.

What unites many minority gun groups in defense of the Second Amendment is that they are not willing to passively place their lives in the hands of the government, particularly given the state's inability to protect the rights of all people at all times in all places. Yes, human beings have a right to "feel safe," and an unalienable right to life. And the best way to ensure those rights is often to entrust individuals to provide for their own defense.

EIGHT

Handgun Ownership Endangers Women

Amnesty International

Amnesty International (AI) is an organization that campaigns for human rights around the world. In the following viewpoint, the organization argues that the presence of firearms increases violence against women. The authors describe how many women are victimized because the men around them have guns. They use guns to intimidate or hurt women, who are helpless to fight back. Another way in which guns negatively affect women is when their husbands or fathers are killed by gun violence, leaving women who depend on these men with an uncertain future. For all of these reasons, the authors conclude that guns endanger women.

"While male-dominated societies often justify small arms possession through the alleged need to protect vulnerable women, women actually face greater danger of violence when their families and communities are armed."

—Barbara Frey, UN Special Rapporteur
on the prevention of human rights violations
committed with small arms and light weapons

Amnesty International, *The Impact of Guns on Women's Lives*, New York, NY: Amnesty International, 2005. Copyright © 2005 Amnesty International, the International Action Network on Small Arms (IANSA) and Oxfam International, 2005. Reproduced by permission.

Domestic–Violence Murders

According to the Bureau of Justice, white females are the most frequent victims of domestic violence - and they are most often killed by guns.

Domestic–Violence Murders by Gender and Race

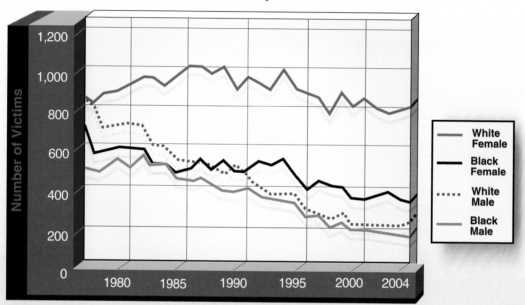

Female Domestic–Violence Victims by Weapon

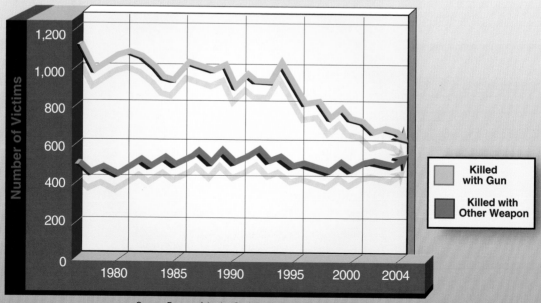

Source: Bureau of Justice Statistics, "Homicide Trends in the U.S.," 2006.

There are estimated to be nearly 650 million small arms in the world today. Nearly 60 per cent of them are in the hands of private individuals—most of them men. And the vast majority of those who make, sell, buy, own, use or misuse small arms are men. What does this mean for the world's women and girls?

This report looks at the impact on women of guns in the home, in communities and during and after conflict. In each of these contexts, it looks at violence committed with guns against women, the role women play in gun use, and the campaigns women are spearheading against gun violence.

More Guns Mean More Danger for Women

Large numbers of women and girls suffer directly and indirectly from armed violence. Women are particularly at risk of certain crimes because of their gender—crimes such as violence in the home and rape. And although available data supports the widespread assumption that most direct casualties of gun violence are men, particularly young men, women suffer disproportionately from firearms violence, given that they are almost never the buyers, owners or users of such weapons.

Guns affect women's lives when they are not directly in the firing line. Women become the main breadwinners and primary carers when male relatives are killed, injured or disabled by gun violence. Women are displaced and forced to flee their homes for an uncertain future. Displaced women often face starvation and disease as they struggle to fend for their families. And women, like men, are caught in the crossfire, both in times of war and of peace.

Violence against women, whether committed with boots or fists or weapons, is rooted in pervasive discrimination which denies women equality with men. It occurs in a variety of contexts and cuts across borders, religions and class. This is not because violence against women is natural or inevitable, but because it has been condoned and tolerated as part of historical or cultural practices for so long. Violence against women in the family and community, and violence against women as a result of state repression or armed conflict, are part of the same continuum: much of the violence that is targeted against women in militarized societies and during armed conflict is an extreme manifestation of the discrimination and abuse that women face in peacetime. Whatever the context or immediate cause of the violence, the presence of guns invariably has the same effect: more guns mean more danger for women.

Violence against women persists in every country and in all sectors of society. When such violence involves the use of weapons specifically designed to cause injury and death and which can fire bullets at high speed from a distance, sometimes at a rate of several bullets per second, then the risk to women's lives increases dramatically.

Women, Men, and Guns

The relationship between women and guns is a complex one. Women are not only killed and injured by the use of weapons, they also play other roles—sometimes as perpetrators of armed violence, sometimes encouraging the use of guns, and sometimes as activists for change.

Women in many countries have become powerful forces for peace and human rights in their communities. This report includes the experiences of women who have been affected by gun violence and have decided to do something about it by calling for tougher arms controls, for safer communities, and for respect for women's human rights. Their campaigns are working to rid not only their own lives, but also those of their families and communities of the ravages of gun violence.

The Myth That Guns Protect

However, women's attitudes can sometimes contribute to the powerful cultural conditioning that equates masculinity with owning and using a gun, and regards gun abuse by men as acceptable. Women sometimes overtly encourage their men to fight, and, more subtly, support the attitudes and stereotypes promoting gun culture. Women and girls also actively participate in many of the world's conflicts, either willingly, through coercion, economic pressure, or because they have been abducted and forced to serve. For some women and girls in armed groups having a gun is seen as a way of protecting themselves and acquiring greater status. However, this is frequently illusory; and many girl and women combatants continue to be abused and are forced to commit abuses themselves.

The perception that a gun provides some measure of protection can be found in many different social contexts and is not confined to situations of armed conflict. Many men carry guns as part of their perceived and constructed role as "protectors" of women; the argument used by gun lobbyists is that they need guns to protect their families from armed intruders or attackers. But the reality of gun ownership and use is very different. Thousands of men in different countries are becoming actively involved in arms control campaigns that try to achieve greater security and safety for everyone and are also joining campaigns to stop violence against women. Some men are working alongside women specifically to challenge existing cultures of masculinity and the presumption that violence, including sexual violence, against women, is "normal" male behaviour.

Campaigns like the White Ribbon campaign, started by men in Canada to challenge men's silent complicity in violence against women, have gained support from men in Costa Rica, Denmark, Mexico, Namibia and South Africa, among other places. At another level, male former combatants and former gang members are among the people who can act most powerfully for change in challenging the links between violent expressions of masculinity and the gun culture. . . .

Armed Violence Against Women

Violence against women in the home has for centuries been regarded as a "private" matter between the abuser, the victim and the immediate family. Women's organizations have been demanding for decades that domestic violence be treated as a crime and a violation of women's human rights.

All over the world, in every class, race and caste, in every reli-
gion and region, there are men who subject their intimate partners to physical or psychological violence, or both. Most violence
against women is committed by the men they live with. The World
Health Organization (WHO) says: "one of the most important
risk factors for women—in terms of their vulnerability to sexual
assault—is being married or cohabiting with a partner". According
to the WHO, refusing sex is one of the reasons women cite most
often as a trigger for violence.

For centuries, women have been told that men have the right
to use violence against them, and many still believe it. Women
in Hawaii describe such violence as "local love. . . more tough
and a little more physical". A 1999 study in South Africa discov-
ered that more than a third of women believe that if a wife does
something wrong her husband has a right to punish her. And a
husband's right to punish his wife is still enshrined in the Penal
Code of Zamfara State, Northern Nigeria, in a section entitled
"Correction of child, pupil, servant or wife".

Guns, Women, and the Home

Family killings are the only category of homicides where women
outnumber men as victims. When a woman is killed in the home,
it is her partner or male relative who is most likely to be the murderer. In 2001 the French Ministry of Health reported that on
average six women a month die at the hands of their current or
former partners. In South Africa, the Medical Research Council
calculates that on average a woman is killed by a current or former partner every six hours. In El Salvador between September
2000 and December 2001, 134 women were murdered; an estimated 98 per cent were killed by their husbands or partners.

The home is traditionally considered to be a safe haven. Yet
this space where women in many societies spend a great deal of
their time, and where they frequently object to the presence of
weapons, exposes them to a particularly high risk of death when
a gun is present. Most of the research available on what increases the risk of a woman being killed in the home has been con-

ducted in countries of the North. Two recent studies from the USA show that:

- several factors affect a woman's chances of being killed by her husband or boyfriend, but *access to a gun* increases the risk five-fold;
- *having a gun in the home* increased the overall risk of someone in the household being murdered by 41 per cent; but for women in particular the risk was nearly tripled (an increase of 272 per cent).

Gun Violence Against Women Around the World

The proportion of domestic homicides involving guns varies across the world. In South Africa and France, one in three women killed by their husbands is shot; in the USA this rises to two in three.

Another study compared female homicide rates with gun ownership levels in 25 high-income countries, and found that where

"Pistol Power," cartoon by Vince O'Farrell. *The Illawarra Mercury*, Australia, January 27, 2004. Copyright © 2004 Vince O'Farrell. All rights reserved. Reproduced by permission of Cagle Cartoons, Inc.

Some believe that a woman's chance of being hurt or killed by a gun increases when a firearm is kept in the home.

firearms are more available, more women are killed. In the USA, where there are high levels of gun ownership, women were at greater risk of homicide. The USA accounted for 32 per cent of the female population in these 25 countries, but for 70 per cent of all female homicides and 84 per cent of all women killed with firearms.

Researchers for the South African Medical Research Council stated that in 1998 the rate of firearms episodes across three South African provinces was 10 times higher than in the USA, and that 150 in every 100,000 women aged between 18 and 49 in these provinces had been the victim of a firearms-related incident.

Reducing a Woman's Ability to Defend Herself

Thus the data show that the involvement of guns makes it far more likely that an attack will prove lethal. Why are guns so deadly in domestic assaults? One reason is the severity of the wounds caused by gunshot which is highly destructive of human tissue. Another reason is that the presence of a firearm, with its threat of lethality, reduces a woman's capacity for resistance. The trauma of being threatened by a husband or partner is all the greater when he brandishes a gun and there is a very real danger of being killed. The wife of a US soldier told researchers: "He would say, 'You will do this, or. . . ', and he would go to the gun cabinet."

Guns also reduce the chances of victims escaping or of outsiders intervening to assist them. This was dramatically demonstrated on 7 August 2004, when 45-year old Marc Cécillon, five times French rugby captain, returned to a party held in his honour in his home town of Bourgoin-Jallieu near Lyon. Shortly before midnight, the hosts' teenage son reportedly saw Marc Cécillon coming up the driveway, tucking a pistol into the waistband of his shorts. The hosts' son ran to warn the guests, but he was too late. In the presence of 60 party-goers, Marc Cécillon approached the table where his wife Chantal was talking to friends and shot her four times with a .359 magnum, killing her instantly.

Chantal Cécillon was killed in public, but the typical domestic killing occurs at the victim's home. Elizabeth Mhlongo of South Africa was shot dead in her bedroom in 1999, along with her five-year-old daughter Tlaleng. Her husband Solomon, a legal gun owner, emptied a magazine of bullets into the two victims, stopped to reload and then continued firing until the gun jammed. Elizabeth was left sprawled at the side of the bed, her chest, head, thigh and hand peppered with bullets, while Tlaleng lay slumped sideways in a blood-spattered chair.

NINE

Increasing Background Checks Will Reduce Violent Crime

Educational Fund to Stop Gun Violence

> In the following viewpoint, the Educational Fund to Stop Gun Violence (EFSGV) argues that increasing background checks of people who buy guns can reduce gun violence. The organization notes that state gun control laws are inconsistent: While some states conduct extensive background checks, many others do not. Therefore, it can be easy for felons, domestic abusers, or other violent people to obtain a gun. The EFSGV concludes that background check laws have failed to keep guns out of the hands of criminals, and that the flow of firearms to those who shouldn't have them can only be stopped by increasing investigations of people who want to buy a gun.

The 1994 Brady Act introduced an essential law enforcement tool to help keep guns out of the hands of criminals: background checks. The checks help prevent the sale of guns to purchasers prohibited by law from owning them (e.g., because of felonies, domestic abuse, or serious mental illness).

Research clearly shows that background checks are effective in blocking criminal access to guns. Nearly 700,000 illegal purchas-

Educational Fund to Stop Gun Violence, *Closing Illegal Gun Markets: Extending Criminal Background Checks to All Gun Sales*, Washington, DC: The Educational Fund to Stop Gun Violence, May 2002. Copyright © 2002 The Educational Fund to Stop Gun Violence. All rights reserved. Reproduced by permission.

es were prevented by Brady Act background checks from 1994 through 2000.

Also, felons, domestic abusers and other prohibited purchasers are less likely to try to buy guns when they know comprehensive background check requirements are in place.

Background Checks Should Be a Part of All Gun Purchases

But current federal law requires criminal background checks only for guns sold through licensed firearm dealers, which account for just 60 percent of gun sales. That means two out of every five guns acquired in the United States—including guns bought at gun shows, through classified ads, and between individuals—change hands without a background check. *Statistical analysis indicates that extending criminal background checks to all gun transactions in the*

President Bill Clinton signs the Brady Act in 1993. The law is named after James Brady (left) who was shot during an assassination attempt on President Ronald Reagan in 1981.

United States could prevent nearly 120,000 additional illegal gun sales every year.

Extending criminal background checks to all gun transactions would allow law-abiding Americans to purchase guns, while providing law enforcement officials with an essential tool to close illegal gun markets and prevent criminal access to guns.

Although 16 states have taken the first steps toward expanding background checks beyond licensed dealers, only a handful of these have implemented truly comprehensive background check systems. California has implemented such a system, and its experience demonstrates the ability of an extended background check system to stop more illegal gun sales.

Lack of Consistent Laws

"Criminals should not be allowed to get guns." This simple, common sense belief is shared by nearly every American, no matter which side of the gun debate he or she agrees with more. It is also the intent of our national gun laws: Convicted felons, domestic

Background Check Denials

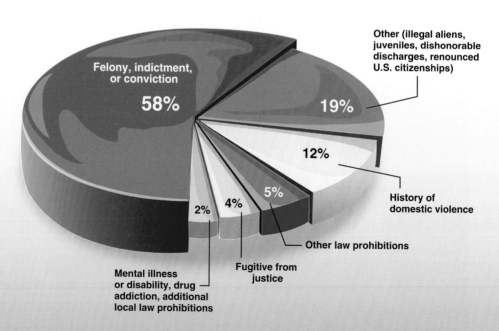

Felony, indictment, or conviction
58%

Other (illegal aliens, juveniles, dishonorable discharges, renounced U.S. citizenships)
19%

12%
History of domestic violence

5%
Other law prohibitions

4%
Fugitive from justice

2%
Mental illness or disability, drug addiction, additional local law prohibitions

Source: Educational Fund to Stop Gun Violence, "Closing Illegal Gun Markets: Extending Criminal Background Checks to All Gun Sales, " May 2002.

abusers, and those with dangerous mental illnesses are among those prohibited from buying or owning guns.

However, the lack of consistent laws means that criminals still do obtain guns, and they do so easily. Federal background checks are required only for gun sales that occur through licensed gun dealers. *The 40 percent of sales that take place outside the network of licensed gun dealers can, under federal law, occur with no background check, no questions asked.*

Background checks are a primary tool used by law enforcement to stop criminals from getting guns. The 1994 Brady Act mandated background checks for sales from licensed gun dealers, such as gun stores. But criminals can avoid gun stores, opting instead to get their guns through *private transactions* between unlicensed sellers, friends, associates, and other informal contacts. Remarkably, federal law does not require a background check for any of these sales.

This report presents a new analysis of the effectiveness of background checks, and recommends their expanded use to stop more criminals from getting guns.

Extending Background Checks Would Prevent Illegal Gun Sales

Extending America's criminal background check system to all gun transactions—and strictly enforcing them—could prevent nearly 120,000 additional illegal gun transactions annually—sales that, under the current system, likely go through undetected.

Between 1999 and 2000, 16.3 million applications for firearm transfers were subject to a background check. About 2.2 percent of these submissions, some 357,000 applications, were rejected because the applicant was a prohibited purchaser.

Researchers estimate, however, that firearms acquired through licensed dealers account for only 60 percent of gun transfers. That means that during the same two years, roughly 10,867,000 additional transactions occurred through non-dealer sales that were *not* subject to background checks. If criminal background checks had been strictly applied to these non-dealer transactions, and if the rejection rate was the same as the rejection rate for dealer sales over the two-year period, an additional 239,000 illegal firearm transactions could have been blocked, an average of almost 120,000 each year.

However, even this significant figure may underestimate the number of illegal gun acquisitions that could be prevented by extending background checks to all sales, because prohibited purchasers may be more likely than legal gun buyers to seek out non-dealers to obtain firearms. If that were so, the rejection rate for non-dealer transactions could be much higher than the rejection rate for dealer sales.

Are Current Laws Working?

Current federal law requires criminal background checks for transactions conducted by federally licensed gun dealers (FFLs)—those who are "engaged in the business" of selling firearms (e.g., gun store owners).

However, individuals who are not "engaged in the business" of selling guns are nonetheless allowed under federal law to sell guns in large quantities from their "private collections." These unlicensed—or private—sellers are not subject to the requirements of licensed dealers, and therefore do not have to conduct background checks on buyers. Some states have established their own background check system for private sales, but most have not. Private sales, which account for an estimated 40 percent of gun sales nationwide, take place at gun shows, through the classified ads, and even over the Internet.

That means that in most states, felons, domestic abusers, and other potentially violent individuals can still get guns easily, no questions asked. . . .

The Stopping Power of Criminal Background Checks

Research clearly shows that background checks help block criminal access to guns. Nearly 700,000 illegal purchases—or 2.3

"Concealed Weapons Permit," cartoon by Mike Keefe. *Denver Post*, May 22, 2003. Copyright ©
2003 Mike Keefe. All rights reserved. Reproduced by permission.

percent of all attempts to buy from licensed dealers—were prevented by Brady Act background checks from 1994 through 2000.
During 2000, most rejections resulted from prior felony convictions or indictments, and nearly 70 percent resulted from either
felonies or histories of domestic violence.

As previously noted, the Brady Act—which had initially
addressed only handguns—was expanded in 1998 to include long-
gun transfers by gun dealers. Prohibited purchaser rejections
jumped from roughly 70,000 total rejections per year from 1996
to 1998, to more than 200,000 in 1999. Had the Brady Act included long guns since 1994, hundreds of thousands of additional illegal transactions could have been prevented.

Furthermore, the lowest rejection rates occur in states with
expanded background check systems, such as New Jersey and

Illinois. Because criminals know the stopping power of comprehensive background check systems, they may be less likely to try to buy guns from licensed dealers in states with stronger systems than in states with less rigorous ones.

Moreover, background checks have proven to be of minimal inconvenience to gun buyers. The General Accounting Office has reported that 95 percent of background checks are completed within two hours, and most are completed in just two minutes.

How Do Criminals Get Guns?

With criminal background checks required for only some gun transactions, criminals still have easy access to guns. Where are they getting them? Research provides a clear answer: Unregulated transactions disproportionately feed the illegal gun market.

- One Bureau of Alcohol, Tobacco, and Firearms (ATF) study examined more than 21,000 crime gun traces—the path of a gun from the time it is legally purchased to its use in crime. Nearly 90 percent of these crime guns had changed hands at least once, after originally being bought at a licensed gun dealer, before being used in a crime.

- In another study, ATF reviewed more than 1,500 gun trafficking investigations conducted during a two-year period. The study found that gun shows and other secondary-market sources—venues for selling weapons after their original purchase—were a "major trafficking channel," involving "approximately 26,000 illegally diverted firearms." Unlicensed, private sellers were responsible for nearly 23,000 illegally trafficked guns. The report notes "investigations usually involve multiple trafficking channels," suggesting that many trafficked guns may involve both a gun show sale and a sale by an unlicensed seller.

- The same ATF study of trafficking investigations found that "the many thousands of guns that traffickers supply illegally, without a Brady background check or [a federal] transfer record that enables tracing, are firearms that are likely to be associated with other crimes." ATF also noted that "persons prohibited from possessing firearms, including felons, are obtaining guns from the illegal market," and that these trafficked firearms "are subsequently used in serious crimes. . . . "

- A recent Department of Justice study found that the percentage of gun-carrying criminals who got their guns from "friends or family" has increased from 34 percent in 1991 to 40 percent in 1997. This finding again suggests that criminals are looking to unlicensed, private sellers.

Criminals get their guns through private sales that do not require background checks. But what happens in a state where background checks are required for all sales, even private ones?

Feasible and Effective Background Checks

California's background check system has prevented thousands of prohibited transactions that likely would have proceeded in any state without such a system. At the same time, the system has not prevented legal purchasers from buying guns. Legitimate private transactions remain rapid and simple in California, but it's harder for prohibited purchasers to get guns.

In 1991, three years before the Brady Act went into effect, California began requiring virtually every gun transaction in the state—even private sales—to be conducted through a licensed dealer or a law enforcement agency. Existing law already required dealers and law enforcement agencies to conduct background checks before transferring any guns. The 1991 law therefore established background checks for all gun sales, including long guns.

According to the California Department of Justice, which administers the state's background check system, 354,202 background checks were conducted in 2001, resulting in just over 3,600 denials. More than 33,500 of these checks involved private transactions, hundreds of which were denied. Although additional prohibited transactions could be blocked if California adopted a more comprehensive registration system, the state's experience

A woman discusses machine guns with a store clerk. Background checks can prevent gun sales to those who are prohibited from purchasing firearms.

demonstrates the value of extending background checks to all transactions.

Still, the additional denied gun transactions in California likely prevented violent crimes in the state, and they demonstrate the stopping power of background checks. When background checks are applied to unregulated gun transactions, more criminals are blocked from getting guns, and potentially deadly crimes are prevented.

The Brady Law requires licensed dealers to conduct a criminal background check before any gun sale can proceed. Since its enactment, the Brady Law has proven to be one of the most efficient law enforcement tools available, preventing nearly 700,000 illegal transactions from occurring through licensed gun dealers.

But the Brady Law's application—and therefore its effectiveness—is limited; the law only applies to transactions by licensed dealers. Forty percent of gun transactions nationwide occur through unlicensed sellers and private transactions that require no background check, no questions asked. This gaping loophole in federal law may explain why nine out of ten traced crime guns have changed hands through at least one private transaction.

In the few states that have extended criminal background checks to cover all guns and all transactions, it is harder for criminals to obtain guns. State officials have found these laws to be a valuable, cost-effective tool, helping police enforce the laws prohibiting criminals and other dangerous people from getting guns. Despite the clear value of extending background checks to all transactions, most states still do not require criminal background checks for sales by unlicensed sellers.

Making Background Checks on All Gun Sales a Reality

An effective and efficient solution to the continued widespread sale of guns to prohibited purchasers would be a federal policy extending criminal background checks for all gun sales. In the absence of a federal standard, states can slow the flow of guns to the illegal gun market by expanding their own background check systems.

Although different proposals may include differing standards and methods of implementation, to be effective, a background check policy should adhere to the following principles:

- The same rules that apply to licensed gun dealer transactions (e.g., waiting periods, transfer requirements, record-keeping) should apply to transactions by unlicensed/private sellers.
- The criminal background check system should apply to all transactions, regardless of where they occur; this would require all gun transactions to take place through a licensed gun dealer, or through a local law enforcement agency.
- Criminal background checks should apply to all modern, functional guns, including handguns, rifles and shotguns.

Extending criminal background checks to all gun sales would still allow law-abiding Americans to purchase guns, while providing law enforcement officials with an essential tool to close illegal gun markets.

TEN

Increasing Background Checks Threatens Gun Owners' Rights

Gun Owners of America

In the following viewpoint, Gun Owners of America, a pro-gun organization, argues that requiring extensive background checks violates the Second Amendment rights of gun owners. Background checks do not keep guns out of criminal hands, the authors reason, because criminals rarely go through legal channels to get guns. Therefore, background checks infringe on the privacy and rights of the most law-abiding gun owners. For these reasons, the authors conclude that background checks are just an excuse for anti-gun advocates to try to make gun ownership illegal.

A convicted armed robber has just been released from prison. He hits the streets, and immediately begins looking for a way to get some cash. He has a decision to make: legitimate work or go back to plying his old trade. He decides to knock off a 7-11.

Of course, he needs a gun, so before heading out to the store he stops by a gun dealer to have his background check done before he purchases a firearm. What's wrong with this picture? Apparently nothing to some politicians in Washington.

Gun Owners of America, "Fact Sheet-Instant Registration Check Threatens Gun Owners' Rights," *Gun Owners of America*, March 2002. Copyright © 2006, 1997–05 by Gun Owners of America. Reproduced by permission.

Making Wrong Assumptions About Criminals

The Brady Instant Registration Check operates under the assumption that criminals willingly submit to police background checks. In reality, the instant check only harasses law-abiding citizens because they are the only ones honest enough to obey the law. Criminals are unaffected; there is no background check on black-market gun purchases.

The "instant check" is proving to be the downfall of the pro-gun movement. "Pro-gun" politicians and organizations have been duped into supporting this dangerous concept, without investigating the inherent problems of a mandatory background check system.

Most gun owners agree that the biggest step toward a complete ban on the private ownership of firearms is the registering of gun owners. Using the so-called instant check system, passed as part of the Brady bill, the federal government has taken a giant leap in that direction.

For years, [Gun Owners of America] has stood virtually alone in opposing the Brady instant check. Because it is supported by many "pro-gun" politicians and other groups, it is helpful to revisit why GOA opposes this legislation, and why it is a threat to the very core of the Second Amendment. . . .

Background Checks Should Be Ruled Unconstitutional

The primary problem with the Instant Registration Check (and the waiting period) is that the Constitution does not delegate authority to Congress to legislate in these areas. Of course, this argument is largely ignored on Capitol Hill, which views the Constitution as an antiquated, irrelevant document.

Thankfully, the U.S. Supreme Court dusted off its copy of the Constitution and issued a rebuke to Congress on a somewhat similar issue in 1995. The case involved a teenager who was convicted in the lower courts for bringing an unloaded gun to school. The facts of the case were clear—the student had broken the federal school zone gun ban. But the Supreme Court declared the law to be unconstitutional, and the student was ultimately exonerated.

The justices said that Congress has no authority to ban firearms around a school, since its powers are strictly limited by Article I, Section 8 of the Constitution. Neither that section, nor any other provision in the Constitution for that matter, gives authority to propose restrictions upon firearms.

Shouldn't this reasoning also apply to background checks? Where does the Constitution give Congress the power to force decent citizens to submit to FBI registration checks before buying firearms? The authority just isn't there.

Rights Are Not Privileges

One must continually remind the Congress that it is severely limited by the Constitution. Congress ought to be concerned with the national defense, coining money, etc. (pursuant to Article 1, Section 8), and then just go home. The Constitution says nothing about mandating background checks on citizens who are trying to exercise their rights.

Crime was always intended to be an issue handled at the state and local level. It should not be a function of the federal government to conduct background checks on gun purchasers. And now, thanks to the Lautenberg gun ban of 1996, authorities have to research even certain misdemeanor convictions of prospective gun purchasers—including offenses as slight as shoving a spouse, spanking a child or shouting too angrily at another family member. Thus, the time and cost for law enforcement to meet Congressional requirements is mushrooming.

But the federalization of crime is not the only problem that comes with a background check. It is blatantly unconstitutional to require citizens to first have to receive the government's permission before being "allowed" to exercise their Second Amendment rights. The instant check turns our "right" into a "privilege."

Second Amendment Protects Individual Rights

The Second Amendment states, in part, that the "right of the people to keep and bear arms shall not be infringed." That means

Some gun ownership advocates argue that background checks violate the Constitutional right to own guns.

no waiting periods, no background checks (a prior restraint), and no taxes, fees or bans. Clearly, this amendment protects against any infringement on the rights of individual citizens—a protection which is undoubtedly what the Founding Fathers had in mind when they referred to "the people."

On this very point, the Supreme Court stated in *U.S. v. Verdugo-Urquidez* (1990) that:

> "The people" seems to have been a term of art employed in select parts of the Constitution. . . . [and] it suggests that "the people" protected by the Fourth Amendment, and by the First and Second Amendments, and to whom rights and powers are reserved in the Ninth and Tenth Amendments, refers to a class of persons who are part of a national community or who have otherwise developed sufficient connection with this country to be considered part of that community.

A gun store clerk checks the background of a customer.

To be sure, honest gun owners should not have to request permission from, or prove their innocence to, the government before exercising a constitutionally guaranteed right—any more than a preacher or journalist should have to prove his worthiness before exercising his First Amendment rights.

Any scheme that violates this principle is just plain wrong. The Brady Instant Check forces law-abiding gun owners to first get permission from government officials before exercising their rights. This kind of infringement would not be tolerated by defenders of the First Amendment. Neither should it be tolerated by Second Amendment advocates. . . .

Instant Gun Owner Registration

In November, 1998, the Brady Law "sunset" into a national instant check. To conduct the instant background check, the name of the firearm's purchaser must now be entered into a computer and checked against criminal, mental illness, and several other records.

The nature of computerized background checks makes registration of gun owners not only possible, but likely. Mike Slavonic, [National Rifle Association] Director and Chairman of the Legislative Committee for the Allegheny County Sportmen's League, correctly stated that the instant background check could be "our downfall." He notes that:

> What most Americans don't know is that . . . the purpose of [the] Brady [Instant Check] could be used to set the stage for national confiscation. Instant check could eventually keep guns out of the hands of everyone by registering everyone who purchases a handgun, rifle and shotgun and who obtained concealed weapons permits in a computerized database. . . .

But why all the fuss about gun owner registration? Quite simply, gun registration has been used—even in this country—to later confiscate firearms. One such instance occurred in New York City just a few years ago.

Firearm Confiscation

It all began with promises made by New York City officials in the mid-1960s. They wanted to register long guns, over the vocal opposition of the city's gun owners. The city fathers promised they would never use such lists to take away firearms from honest citizens. But in 1991, the city banned (and soon began confiscating) many of those very guns.

Gun owners were ordered to get rid of their newly-banned firearms. Those who didn't comply were subject to having their firearms taken away.

For example, the *Daily News* reported in 1992 that "police raided the home of a Staten Island man who refused to comply with the city's tough ban on assault weapons, and seized an arsenal of firearms. . . . Spot checks are planned [for other homes.]"

New York City officials do not hold a monopoly when it comes to showing bad faith.

California passed a ban on certain semi-automatic firearms in 1989. Banned guns could be legally possessed if they were registered prior to the ban. In the spring of 1995, one man who wished to move to California asked the Attorney General whether his SKS Sporter rifle would be legal in the state. The citizen was assured the rifle was legal, and based on that information, he subsequently moved into the state. But in 1998, California officials reversed course and confiscated the firearm.

Since then, documents leaked from the office of the California Attorney General have showed that state officials were planning a mass-confiscation of privately owned firearms from citizens who had previously registered their guns. . . .

Despite the good faith shown by gun owners, the California government later ordered these gun owners to dispose of their weapons. How did the authorities know whom to contact to notify them to turn in their weapons? The registration lists, of course.

This proves the point that the ultimate goal of registration is to facilitate confiscation.

Not surprisingly, gun registration has also led to confiscation in several places outside of the United States, including Greece, Ireland, Jamaica and Bermuda.

A police officer confiscates guns from a home. Some are concerned that gun registration increases the chances of this happening to gun owners who have not violated any laws.

More recently, full-fledged confiscation of firearms has taken place in England and Australia. Gun bans that were passed in 1997 resulted in massive turn-ins of firearms. . . .

Good Reason to Be Wary

For this reason, many gun owners in the United States are wary of the Brady instant check, as it certainly gives government officials the means of compiling a registration list. And to what end? Will gun owner registration help police solve murder mysteries?

Well, if the experience from Hawaii is any indicator, the answer is a resounding "NO!" Police have spent tens of thousands of man-hours administering licensing and registration laws, but there has not even been a single case where police claim these laws have served to identify a criminal.

Again, here we have gun control laws that do nothing to help catch criminals, but only focus their evil fangs on decent citizens who have committed no crimes.

Gun Control and Genocide

As bad as the five-day waiting period was, the danger it posed was far less than that of the Instant Registration Check. The Brady Instant Registration Check is the foundation for a national, centralized, computerized registration list of gun owners. And the lessons to be learned from countries abroad show that registration is a disease that must be avoided like the plague.

In an exhaustive study on the subject of foreign gun control, Jews for the Preservation of Firearms Ownership has researched and translated several gun control laws from other countries. Their publication, *Lethal Laws: "Gun Control" is the Key to Genocide*, documents how gun control (and confiscation) has preceded the slaughter and genocide of millions of people in Turkey, the Soviet Union, Germany, China, Cambodia and other countries.

Once the identification of gun owners is in place (registration), the thugs in power (a.k.a. the government) confiscated firearms. In Rwanda, they also confiscated machetes. Then the slaughter of the target population began—Jews in Nazi Germany, Ukrainians and others in Soviet Russia, Christians in Uganda, Indians in Guatemala, the educated in Cambodia and so forth.

This is not to say that genocide *must* follow the confiscation of firearms—just like the removing of a fire extinguisher from a home does not mean the house *must* catch on fire.

History teaches, however, that guns (like fire extinguishers) are effective insurance policies. Many problems could have been prevented if decent people had the freedom to choose the best "insurance" available to them. And many people could have retained their "insurance" if they had never been registered in the first place.

The figures are in. During the past century alone, governments have slaughtered their tens of millions, the Al Capones their scores and hundreds. Yet Sarah Brady, Sen. Charles Schumer (D-NY) and the other advocates of civilian disarmament breeze right on past the killing fields of our recent past. They also overlook the massive threat to personal security posed by center-city street gangs.

Instead, their desire is to convince us all that it is the guns of the victims that are at fault—decent people wishing to protect themselves from the criminals set loose on our streets by our government. We are watching a monumental shifting of the blame from those who have brought us a failed system of criminal justice. They want us to look not at murderers put out on the street. Rather than blame murderers, "blame guns" we are told.

Gun Control Laws Are Dangerous

Our answer to the civilian disarmament crowd has to be that crime is their fault, not the fault of gun owners. Gun control laws kill. When stating our position, we must not fall into the trap of agreeing to policies, such as the Instant Registration Check, that make disarmament possible. We should press on for what we want—the free exercise of a constitutionally protected right to keep and bear arms. After all, we will never get more than we ask for.

Gun controllers are the friends of criminals and the enemies of freedom. They arrogantly assume that only they (and their buddies in the government) are responsible enough to be trusted with guns. The watchword should be that guns save lives, gun control kills. And the Instant Registration Check is gun control—a threat to every citizen.

ELEVEN

Improving Gun Design Can Reduce Gun Violence

Julie Samia Mair, Stephen Teret, and Shannon Frattaroli

> In the following viewpoint, Julie Samia Mair, Stephen Teret, and Shannon Frattaroli argue that better-designed guns could play an important role in reducing gun violence. Firearms equipped with better safety features, such as loaded-chamber indicators and Smart Gun technology, would prevent unauthorized users from firing a gun. The authors reason that it is easier to modify gun design than improve human behavior to ensure people act responsibly with guns. Julie Samia Mair and Shannon Frattaroli are assistant scientists at the Health Policy and Management Department at Johns Hopkins University in Baltimore. Stephen Teret is the director of the Center for Law and the Public's Health at Johns Hopkins.

Gun violence is a public health problem. Each year in the United States, tens of thousands of people are killed by gunfire and many more are seriously injured with resulting disabilities. Among the victims of gun violence are curious young children who encounter loaded guns and do not understand the damage they can cause; depressed teenagers who commit suicide; victims of domestic abuse; and the casualties of many other vio-

Julie Samia Mair, Stephen Teret, and Shannon Frattaroli, *Suing the Gun Industry: A Battle at the Crossroads of Gun Control and Mass Torts*, Ann Arbor, MI: University of Michigan Press, 2005. Copyright © by the University of Michigan 2005. All rights reserved. Reproduced by permission.

lent crimes. For some population groups, death by gunfire is the number one cause of death. It has been estimated that the lifetime medical costs of gun violence that occurred in the single year of 1994 was approximately $2.3 billion, a huge sum of money that could be better spent on solving other societal ills. Whether measured by mortality or morbidity statistics, by cost to society, or by sheer grief and disruption to the population, the toll of gun violence is too high, and it places the public's safety at unacceptable levels of risk. Interventions are needed to address this public health problem.

Although guns and gun violence have long been a part of American life, it is only in the past few decades that guns and

Homicide by Weapon Type

Handguns are the number one weapon used to commit murder in the United States.

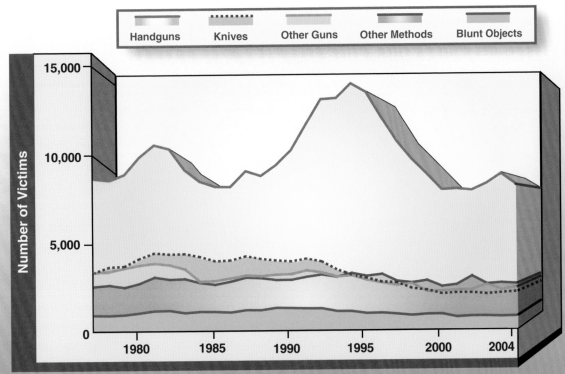

Source: Bureau of Justice Statistics, "Homicide Trends in the U.S.," 2006.

gun-related injuries have come to be seen as a public health issue. . . .

Fix by Design, Not Behavior Modification

Two of the principles that help define the discipline of public health are as follows: (1) preventing damage to humans by injury and disease is preferable to repairing damage after it has occurred; and (2) prevention is best accomplished by protection that is provided automatically on a population basis and does not require each individual to always act carefully. This is why we fluoridate water supplies to reduce the risk incidence of dental caries rather than ask each individual to remember to consume a certain amount of fluorine each day. We regulate the design of products for safety, such as specifying certain dimensions for baby cribs to reduce the risk to infants of strangulation rather than asking parents to choose their cribs carefully and always to monitor their sleeping babies. Applying this approach to the area of gun violence, it is considered more effective and therefore preferable to address the design of guns before they get into the hands of millions of people rather than rely on our ability to control the behaviors of those millions so that they always act prudently once the guns are in their hands.

Safe design can be mandated by government regulations. For most consumer products, the nation's Consumer Product Safety Commission (CPSC) has the responsibility to protect the public from unsafe designs. But regarding guns, the CPSC has been expressly forbidden by Congress to regulate design safety. In fact, no federal agency comprehensively regulates the safe design of firearms, despite the fact that guns are the second leading cause of injury deaths in the United States. Guns, and particularly handguns, could be designed more safely by the use of existing, inexpensive technologies, resulting in a saving of lives. Gun manufacturers have been reluctant to use some of these technologies and have been adamant in their opposition to any regulations that could require safer guns.

Safety Devices Could Be Installed

Two examples of existing technologies that would likely save lives if they were used uniformly on all handguns are loaded chamber indicators and magazine safety devices. A loaded chamber indicator lets the person holding a gun know whether there is a bullet in the chamber, just like a camera lets the user know if it is loaded with film. Its purpose is to help prevent an unintentional discharge of the gun, which has been known to result in death. A magazine safety prevents a pistol from being fired if the magazine or clip, in which the ammunition is stored, has been removed from the pistol. Again, deaths have resulted from people believing a gun was unloaded and then pulling the trigger. A magazine safety is important because some people think that, once they remove the magazine, all of the ammunition has been removed; however, often a bullet remains in the chamber of the gun, and if the trigger is pulled on a pistol without a magazine safety, that bullet will be discharged. In a 1997 nationally representative survey, over one-third of respondents either erroneously believed that a pistol could not be fired with its ammunition magazine removed (20.1 percent) or did not know (14.5 percent). Of this one-third, 28 percent lived in homes with guns.

The technologies for loaded chamber indicators and magazine safeties have existed since the early twentieth century, and the cost of these safety devices is minimal. But the vast majority of pistol models presently being sold do not include these safety devices. Some manufacturers provide the safety devices on some of their models but not others. This is akin to a car manufacturer offering seatbelts on some models but not others—a behavior that would be illegal, due to federal safety regulations for motor vehicles.

Smart Gun Technology

Another important design feature that would materially enhance the safety of guns is the use of a technology that discriminates between authorized users of a gun and unauthorized users. Every year, many die from homicides, suicides, or unintended deaths when a gun is operated by an unauthorized user. This could be a criminal who stole a gun or bought a stolen gun from another, a depressed teenager using the gun for suicide, or a curious young child who does not understand the dangers presented by guns. Many of these deaths could be averted if the gun was made so that it was personalized or operable only by certain authorized users. Personalization of guns can be accomplished by the use of locks built into the gun itself or by technologies that recognize the biometrics of the authorized users. A few gun makers, such as Taurus, now offer some forms of personalization based on internal locking devices, but most newly made handguns are as easily operated by a thief or young child as by the owner.

Cook and Ludwig analyzed the cost-effectiveness of personalized technology and found that the benefits associated with requiring personalized technology on new guns should more than outweigh the costs. . . .

A Public Duty

The commitment of public health is to determine, through scientific investigation, the risks to the public's well-being and the best ways to reduce those risks. Once the risks and the effective prevention strategies are identified, public health seeks to implement those strategies through policies, educational programs, and advocacy. Some risks are easier to identify than others. For example, it took substantial efforts over a long period of time to prove the causal connections between tobacco products and certain diseases such as lung cancer. With guns, the causal connection between being shot and being at risk of death is readily apparent. The design interventions discussed in this chapter address the undisputed causal connection between guns (a manufactured product designed to inflict injury) and gun injury independent of a relationship between population level availability and violence. An individual with a bullet wound suffers that injury, on the most basic level, as a result of a gun having been

Gun locks can prevent accidental shootings.

successfully discharged. Similarly, distribution strategies are designed to limit gun access to agreed-upon high-risk users, such as convicted felons and youth, irrespective of general availability. The proper intervention for reducing the nation's toll of gun-related deaths, however, is a subject of considerable

Diagram of Oxford Micro
ces' A236 Parallel DSP Chip

Steven Morton, president of Oxford Micro Device Inc., holds a hand gun that uses a computer chip that recognizes the fingerprints of the gun's authorized user.

controversy. There are some (generally not working in the field of public health) who argue that more guns would mean fewer gun-related deaths. Although beyond the scope of this chapter, this assertion has been met with substantial criticism, mostly regarding the research methodology used in reaching this conclusion. The weight of public health research finds that the high prevalence of guns in the United States is associated with this country's high gun death rate and that changing the current practices of gun design and distribution could likely reduce the gun violence problems we face.

What You Should Know About Gun Violence

Facts About Gun Violence in the United States

- The American firearms industry estimates that there are approximately 200 million firearms in the United States; 60–65 million of these are handguns.
- There are approximately one million semiautomatic assault weapons in private hands in the United States, according to the Federal Bureau of Alcohol, Tobacco, and Firearms.
- According to the National Center for Injury Prevention and Control, firearms were involved in 30,136 deaths in the United States in 2003; approximately one-third of these (11,920) were homicides; over one-half (16,970) were suicides.
- According to the *Journal of Trauma*, handguns account for over two-thirds of all firearm-related deaths each year.
- The Colorado Division of Criminal Justice reports that there have been over 28,000 firearm deaths in the United States per year since 1972.
- According to the Centers for Disease Control and Prevention (CDC), firearm injuries are the second leading cause of injury-related deaths in the United States, surpassed only by motor vehicle injuries.
- The National Center for Injury Prevention and Control found that firearms were involved in 64,389 nonfatal injuries in 2004.
- According to the American Psychological Association, firearm homicide is the primary cause of death for African Americans between the ages of 15 and 34.

- Violating a federal firearms law can result in a fine as high as $250,000, as well as incarceration.
- According to the Bureau of Justice Statistics (BJS), fatal firearm crime rates have declined since 1994, reaching the lowest level ever recorded in 2004.

Facts About International Gun Violence

Facts gathered from Wendy Cukier and Victor W. Sidel's *The Global Gun Epidemic: From Saturday Night Specials to AK-47s*:

- An estimated 200,000 persons are killed each year by firearm violence around the world, including homicides, suicides, and accidents.
- Firearm death rates, including homicides, suicides, and accidents, vary widely from country to country:
  - United States 10.27 per 100,000 persons.
  - Puerto Rico 19.12 per 100,000 persons.
  - Germany 1.34 per 100,000 persons.
  - El Salvador 25.8 per 100,000 persons.
  - Japan .06 per 100,000 persons.
- North, Central, and South America have 14% of the world's population and over 50% of the world's nonmilitary-related firearm deaths.
- The United States manufactures 50% of the world's firearms; France and England, 10% each; Germany, Russia, and Japan, 4% each.

Facts About Gun Violence: Children and Adolescents

- An average eight youths 19 or younger die of gunshot wounds each day in the United States, according to the American Academy of Pediatrics.
- According to the Children's Defense Fund and National Center for Health Statistics, for each firearm death, four or five more children are injured.
- The National Vital Statistics System reports that more youths commit suicide with firearms than by any other method. This is true for both males and females, younger and older adolescents, and for all races.

- The Youth Handgun Safety Act of 1994 prohibits possession of handguns by anyone under the age of 18 (United States Department of Justice).

According to the Centers for Disease Control and Prevention (CDC):

- In 2003, 5,570 young people between the ages of 10 and 24 were murdered—an average of 15 each day; 82% were killed with firearms.
- In 2003, 2,849 children and teenagers died of firearm injuries, including 1,844 homicides, 810 suicides, and 195 unintentional shootings.
- In 2003, homicide was the second leading cause of death for 15- to 24-year-olds; 82% of these homicides were firearm related.
- In 2003, homicide was the fifth leading cause of death for 10- to 14-year-olds; 69% of these homicides were firearm related.
- 6.1% of high school students reported carrying a gun at least once during the previous 30 days. Male students (10.2%) were significantly more likely than females (1.6%) to have carried a gun.
- School-associated violent deaths account for less than 1% of homicides among school-aged children and youth.

Facts About the Economics of Gun Violence

According to the Brady Center to Prevent Gun Violence:

- The direct and indirect costs of gun violence in the United States have been estimated at $100 billion per year.
- Direct costs include:
  - $22,400 for each unintentional shooting.
  - $18,400 for each gun assault injury.
  - $5,400 for each gun-related suicide.
- Indirect costs include:
  - $2.8 million per firearm fatality.
  - $249,000 per firearm injury requiring hospitalization.
  - $73,000 per firearm injury requiring an emergency room visit.
- In firearm-related injuries, taxpayers shoulder over 85% of the medical costs.

Facts About Women and Gun Violence

According to the Family Violence Prevention Fund:

- Nearly one-third of all women murdered in the United States are murdered by a current or former intimate partner; of females killed with a firearm, almost two-thirds are killed by their intimate partners.
- In 2002 in the United States, 54% of female homicide victims were shot and killed with a gun.
- In 2002 in the United States, handguns were used in 73% of cases where men used firearms to kill women.

The International Action Network on Small Arms reports that:

- In South Africa, a woman is killed by a current or former partner every 18 hours.
- In the United States, a gun in the home increases the risk that someone in the household will be murdered by 41%; a gun in the home increases the risk for women by 272%.
- In France and South Africa, one in every three women killed by their husbands are shot; in the United States, two in three women killed by their husbands are shot.
- In family homicides, women outnumber men as victims; the murderer is most often her male partner or male relative.

What You Should Do About It: Living with Firearms

With over three thousand teens killed in firearm-related deaths each year in the United States, and four to five times that number suffering from firearm-related injuries, it is clear that firearms, when handled improperly, can be dangerous. Since there are as many as 200 million rifles, shotguns, and handguns owned by about 100 million Americans, many people who do not own firearms themselves nevertheless are likely to come into contact with rifles or handguns at a friend or relative's home. With so many firearms present in the United States, it is important to understand both the legal issues surrounding firearms and vital safety precautions. It is also important to know what steps to take when someone is using a firearm improperly or illegally.

Federal Firearm Laws

Who can and cannot own a gun in the United States? There are literally thousands of local, state, and federal laws concerning guns in the United States, and what may be legal in one state (carrying a concealed weapon, for example), may be illegal in another. Federal laws, however, set a number of general guidelines. A U.S. citizen must be twenty-one to buy a handgun or handgun ammunition; a citizen must be eighteen to purchase a rifle or shotgun. It is illegal to provide a handgun or ammunition to minors (anyone under eighteen). It is also illegal for the following persons to own guns:

- Anyone convicted of a misdemeanor crime of domestic violence.
- Convicted felons.
- Illegal aliens.

- Fugitives from justice.
- A person dishonorably discharged from the army.
- A person who has renounced his or her citizenship.

Federal penalties for illegal firearm activities include:
- A five-year sentence for the use of a firearm in a drug-related crime.
- A ten-year sentence for knowingly transferring a firearm used to commit a felony.
- A ten-year sentence for anyone who alters a semiautomatic weapon into a fully automatic weapon.
- A ten-year sentence for convicted felons possessing a firearm.

In addition to incarceration, violating a federal firearms law can result in fines as high as $250,000. The Brady Bill, passed into law in 1994, requires background checks for all individuals who purchase a firearm.

Firearm Safety

What safety precautions should an adult take when keeping firearms in the home? What safety precautions should a child or young adult take if he or she finds a firearm in the home? And, what safety precautions should a child, young adult, or adult take in using a firearm for target practice or hunting?

The most important safety practice an adult gun owner can follow is properly storing any firearm. Storing a firearm in a shoebox at the top of the closet is not safe; at most, this only keeps the gun out of reach of very young children. Instead, a firearm should be stored in a gun safe or locked cabinet, unloaded; the ammunition should be stored and locked separately. Other important safety measures include:

- A gunlock or trigger lock that can prevent a gun from firing.
- Keys to gun safes and locked cabinets should be stored to prevent access.
- Children should be taught never to handle guns without adult supervision.

Despite the importance of these essential safety rules, many firearm owners fail to follow them. This means that children and young adults often find firearms in the home. "Most gunshot injuries happen after kids discover loaded guns at home," notes *Kids Health*. Many people are unaware that approximately 25% of 3- to 4-year-olds possess the physical strength to pull a trigger and fire a gun. *Kids Health* states that it is essential for children and young adults to understand and follow these steps if they find a firearm:

- Stop.
- Don't touch.
- Remove yourself from the area.
- Tell an adult.

Many children and adolescents are given permission by an adult to handle rifles and shotguns for the purpose of hunting and/or target practice. Even with permission to use a firearm, proper handling and use are essential to the safety of the firearm user and anyone else who may be in the vicinity. The following safety steps apply to anyone handling a firearm, whether a minor or an adult:

- Firearms should always be treated as though they are loaded; never point a firearm at another person.
- Never place your finger on the trigger until you are ready to fire.
- Always be aware of your target and alert to your surroundings.

Firearm Intervention

Although most firearms in America are legally owned, and most Americans follow firearm safety rules, many individuals ignore both the law and safety. Each year, a number of children and young adults choose to carry a firearm illegally, either buying one on the black market or stealing one from someone's home. A number of persons will use these guns to commit robberies, school shootings, and homicides. Others will use them to commit suicide. What should an individual do if he or she knows someone—an acquaintance, relative, or friend—is breaking firearm laws? Is talking about bringing a firearm to school the same thing as bringing a firearm to school? And does it betray a friend's trust to report an illegal firearm to school authorities or the police?

When a child or a young adult possesses an illegal firearm, it is a serious matter that should be handled promptly. Even if the individual never plans to use the firearm, the fact that he or she possesses the gun creates a potential to harm others or the user, perhaps accidentally. Speaking or bragging about carrying a firearm to a prohibited site such as school is also a very serious matter. Even if the individual does not carry out his or her boast or threat, the fact that a boast or threat is made to bring a gun to a school or workplace is a signal that adult intervention is necessary. If you worry that you are betraying a friend by speaking to a guidance counselor or police officer, consider that 1) you are protecting both yourself and others from possible firearm injury and 2) you are protecting your friend from possible injury and the serious consequences of any crime committed.

Used unsafely and illegally, guns have a great potential to harm both the individuals who use them and society at large. By obeying federal and state laws, and following established safety rules, the threat from firearms can be minimized.

ORGANIZATIONS TO CONTACT

The editors have compiled the following list of organizations concerned with the issues debated in this book. The descriptions are derived from materials provided by the organizations. All have publications or information available for interested readers. The list was compiled on the date of publication of the present volume; information provided here may change. Be aware that many organizations take several weeks or longer to respond to inquiries, so allow as much time as possible.

American Civil Liberties Union (ACLU)
132 W. 43rd St.
New York, NY 10036
(212) 944-9800
fax: (212) 869-9065
Web site: www.aclu.org

The ACLU champions the rights set forth in the Declaration of Independence and the U.S. Constitution. It opposes the suppression of individual rights. The ACLU interprets the Second Amendment as a guarantee for states to form militias, not as a guarantee of the individual right to own and bear firearms. Consequently, the organization believes that gun control is constitutional and that because guns are dangerous, gun control is necessary. The ACLU publishes the semiannual *Civil Liberties* in addition to policy statements and reports.

Cato Institute
1000 Massachusetts Ave. NW
Washington, DC 20001
(202) 842-0200
fax: (202) 842-3490
Web site: www.cato.org

The Cato Institute is a libertarian public-policy research foundation. It evaluates government policies and offers reform proposals and commentary on its Web site. Its publications include the Cato Policy Analysis series of reports, which have covered topics such as "Fighting Back: Crime, Self-Defense, and the Right to Carry a Handgun," and "Trust the People: The Case Against Gun Control." It also publishes the magazine *Regulation*, the *Cato Policy Report*, and books such as *The Samurai, The Mountie, and The Cowboy: Should America Adopt the Gun Controls of Other Democracies?*

Center to Prevent Handgun Violence
1250 Eye Street NW, Suite 1100
Washington, DC 20005
(202) 289-7319
fax: (202) 408-1851
Web sites: www.cphv.org
www.gunlawsuits.com

The center is the legal action, research, and education affiliate of Handgun Control, Inc. The center's Legal Action Project provides free legal representation for victims in lawsuits against reckless gun manufacturers, dealers, and owners. The center's Straight Talk About Risks (STAR) program is a violence prevention program designed to help youth develop victim prevention skills and to rehearse behaviors needed to manage conflicts without violence or guns. Its Web sites provide fact sheets and updates on pending gun lawsuits.

Citizens Committee for the Right to Keep and Bear Arms
12500 NE Tenth Pl.
Bellevue, WA 98005
(425) 454-4911
fax: (425) 451-3959
Web site: www.ccrkba.org

The committee believes that the U.S. Constitution's Second Amendment guarantees and protects the right of individual

Americans to own guns. It works to educate the public concerning this right and to lobby legislators to prevent the passage of gun control laws. The committee is affiliated with the Second Amendment Foundation and reports more than six hundred thousand members. It publishes the books *Gun Laws of America, Gun Rights Fact Book, Origin of the Second Amendment,* and *Point Blank: Guns and Violence in America.*

Coalition for Gun Control
P.O. Box 90062, 1488 Queen St. W
Toronto, Ontario M6K 3K3
(416) 604-0209
Web site: www.guncontrol.ca

The coalition was formed to reduce gun death, injury, and crime. It supports the registration of all guns and works for tougher restrictions on handguns. The organization promotes safe storage requirements for all firearms and educates to counter the romance of guns. Various fact sheets and other educational materials on gun control are available on its Web site.

Coalition to Stop Gun Violence
1023 15th St. NW, Suite 301
Washington, DC 20005
(202) 408-0061
Web site: www.csgv.org

The coalition lobbies at the local, state, and federal levels to ban the sale of handguns and assault weapons to individuals and to institute licensing and registration of all firearms. It also litigates cases against firearm makers. Its publications include various informational sheets on gun violence and the *Annual Citizens' Conference to Stop Gun Violence Briefing Book,* a compendium of gun control fact sheets, arguments, and resources.

Doctors for Responsible Gun Ownership
The Claremont Institute
937 West Foothill Blvd., Suite E

Claremont, CA 91711
(909) 621-6825
fax: (909) 626-8724
Web site: www.claremont.org

The organization comprises health-care professionals who oppose gun control. It works to correct what it identifies as poor medical scholarship about the dangers of guns and to educate people on the importance of guns for self-defense. The organization has legally challenged laws that regulate guns. Its publications include the booklet *Firearms: A Handbook for Health Officials*.

Handgun Control, Inc.
1225 Eye St. NW, Suite 1100
Washington, DC 20005
(202) 898-0792
fax: (202) 371-9615
Web site: www.handguncontrol.org

A citizens lobby working for the federal regulation of the manufacture, sale, and civilian possession of handguns and automatic weapons, the organization successfully promoted the passage of the Brady law, which mandates a five-day waiting period for the purchase of handguns. The lobby publishes the quarterly newsletter *Progress Report* and the book *Guns Don't Die—People Do*, as well as legislative reports and pamphlets.

Independence Institute
13952 Denver West Pkwy., Suite 400
Golden, CO 80401
(303) 279-6536
fax: (303) 279-4176
Web site: www.i2i.org

The institute is a pro–free market think tank that supports gun ownership as a civil liberty and a constitutional right. Its publications include books and booklets opposing gun control, such as "Children and Guns: Sensible Solutions," "'Shall Issue': The New Wave of Concealed Handgun Permit Laws," and "Unfair and

Unconstitutional: The New Federal Gun Control and Juvenile Crime Proposals," as well as the book *Guns: Who Should Have Them?* Its Web site also contains articles, fact sheets, and commentary from a variety of sources.

Jews for the Preservation of Firearms Ownership (JPFO)
P.O. Box 270143
Hartford, WI 53207
(262) 673-9745
fax: (262) 673-9746
Web site: www.jpfo.org

JPFO is an educational organization that believes Jewish law mandates self-defense including firearm use. Its primary goal is the elimination of the idea that gun control is a socially useful public policy in any country. JPFO publishes the quarterly *Firearms Sentinel*, the booklet "Will 'Gun Control' Make You Safer?" and regular news alerts.

Join Together
One Appleton St., 4th Floor
Boston, MA 02116-5223
(617) 437-1500
fax: (617) 437-9394
Web site: www.jointogether.org
e-mail: info@jointogether.org

Join Together, a project of the Boston University School of Public Health, is an organization that serves as a national resource for communities working to reduce substance abuse and gun violence. Its publications include a quarterly newsletter.

Million Mom March Foundation
1250 Eye Street NW, Suite 1100
Washington, DC 20005
(888) 989-MOMS
fax: (202) 408-1851

Web site: www.millionmommarch.org
e-mail: national@millionmommarch.org

The foundation is a grassroots organization that supports commonsense gun laws. The foundation organized the Million Mom March, in which thousands marched through Washington, DC, on Mother's Day, May 14, 2000, in support of licensing and registration and other firearms regulations. The foundation's Web site provides fact sheets on gun violence and gun control initiatives.

National Crime Prevention Council (NCPC)

1000 Connecticut Ave. NW, 13th Floor
Washington, DC 20036
(202) 466-6272
fax: (202) 296-1356
Web site: www.ncpc.org

The NCPC is a branch of the U.S. Department of Justice. Through its programs and educational materials, the council works to teach Americans how to reduce crime and to address its causes. It provides readers with information on gun control and gun violence. NCPC's publications include the newsletter *Catalyst*, which is published ten times a year, and the book *Reducing Gun Violence: What Communities Can Do*.

National Institute of Justice (NIJ)
National Criminal Justice Reference Service (NCJRS)

Box 6000
Rockville, MD 20849
(301) 519-3420
(800) 851-5212
Web site: www.ncjrs.org

A component of the Office of Justice Programs of the U.S. Department of Justice, the NIJ supports research on crime, criminal behavior, and crime prevention. The National Criminal Justice Reference Service acts as a clearinghouse that provides information and research about criminal justice. Its publications include the research briefs "Reducing Youth Gun Violence: An Overview of Programs and Initiatives," "Impacts of the 1994 Assault Weapons Ban," and "Homicide in Eight U.S. Cities: Trends, Context, and Policy Implications."

National Rifle Association of America (NRA)
11250 Waples Mill Rd.
Fairfax, VA 22030
(703) 267-1000
fax: (703) 267-3989
Web site: www.nra.org

With nearly 3 million members, the NRA is America's largest organization of gun owners. It is also the primary lobbying group for those who oppose gun control laws. The NRA believes that such laws violate the U.S. Constitution and do nothing to reduce crime. In addition to its monthly magazines *America's 1st Freedom, American Rifleman, American Hunter, Insights,* and *Shooting Sports USA,* the NRA publishes numerous books, bibliographies, reports, and pamphlets on gun ownership, gun safety, and gun control.

Second Amendment Foundation
12500 NE Tenth Pl.
Bellevue, WA 98005
(425) 454-7012
fax: (425) 451-3959
Web site: www.saf.org

The foundation is dedicated to informing Americans about their Second Amendment right to keep and bear firearms. It believes that gun control laws violate this right. The foundation publishes numerous books, including *The Amazing Vanishing Second Amendment; The Best Defense: True Stories of Intended Victims Who Defended Themselves with a Firearm;* and CCW: *Carrying Concealed Weapons.* The complete text of the book *How to Defend Your Gun Rights* is available on its Web site.

U.S. Department of Justice
Office of Justice Programs
950 Pennsylvania Ave. NW
Washington, DC 20530-0001
(202) 514-2000
Web sites: www.usdoj.gov
www.ojp.usdoj.gov/bjs/welcome.html

The Department of Justice protects citizens by maintaining effective law enforcement, crime prevention, crime detection, and prosecution and rehabilitation of offenders. Through its Office of Justice Programs, the department operates the National Institute of Justice, the Office of Juvenile Justice and Delinquency Prevention, and the Bureau of Justice Statistics. Its publications include fact sheets, research packets, bibliographies, and the semi-annual journal *Juvenile Justice*.

Violence Policy Center
1730 Rhode Island Ave. NW, Suite 1014
Washington, DC 20036
(202) 822-8200
fax: (202) 822-8202
Web site: www.vpc.org

The center is an educational foundation that conducts research on firearms violence. It works to educate the public concerning the dangers of guns and supports gun control measures. The center's publications include the report *Handgun Licensing and Registration: What It Can and Cannot Do*; *GUNLAND USA: A State-by-State Ranking of Gun Shows, Gun Retailers, Machine Guns, and Gun Manufacturers*; and *Guns for Felons: How the NRA Works to Rearm Criminals*.

BIBLIOGRAPHY

Books

Massad Ayoob, *The Truth About Self Protection*. Concord, NH: Police Bookshelf, March 2004.

Philip J. Cook and Jens Ludwig, *Gun Violence: The Real Costs*. New York: Oxford University Press, 2002.

Saul Cornell, *A Well-Regulated Militia: The Founding Fathers and the Origins of Gun Control in America*. New York: Oxford University Press, 2006.

David Hemenway, *Private Guns, Public Health*. Ann Arbor: University of Michigan Press, 2004.

James B. Jacobs, *Can Gun Control Work?* New York: Oxford University Press, 2004.

Gary Kleck, *Point Blank: Guns and Violence in America*. Piscataway, NJ: Aldine Transaction, 2005.

Abigail A. Kohn, *Shooters: Myths and Realities of America's Gun Cultures*. New York: Oxford University Press, 2004.

Wayne LaPierre, *The Global War on Your Guns: Inside the UN Plan to Destroy the Bill of Rights*. Nashville, TN: Nelson Current, 2006.

Jens Ludwig and Philip J. Cook, eds., *Evaluating Gun Policy: Effects on Crime and Violence*. Washington, DC: Brookings Institution Press, 2003.

Joyce Lee Malcolm, *Guns and Violence: The English Experience*. Cambridge, MA: Harvard University Press, 2004.

Andrew J. McClurg, David B. Kopel, and Brannon P. Denning, eds., *Gun Control and Gun Rights: A Reader and Guide*. New York: New York University Press, 2002.

Robert J. Spitzer, *The Politics of Gun Control*. 3rd ed. Washington, DC: CQ Press, 2003.

Periodicals

Capital Times, "Timid Congress Forces Mayors to Move on Guns," May 1, 2006.

Hector Castro, "Police Chief Reacts to Shootings: He Cites Easy Access to Guns, Limited Mental Health Care," *Seattle Post-Intelligencer,* April 25, 2006.

Christian Science Monitor, "Is Self-Defense Law Vigilante Justice? Some Say Proposed Laws Can Help Deter Gun Violence. Others Worry About Deadly Confrontations," February 4, 2006.

Crime Control Digest, "Boston Opens Center to Curb Gun Violence," November 4, 2005.

———, "Connecticut Hits Guns in Anti-Violence Drive," February 24, 2006.

Vanessa Farr, "The New War Zone: The Ubiquitous Presence of Guns and Light Weapons Has Changed the Definitions of 'War,' 'Victim,' and 'Perpetrator,'" *Women's Review of Books,* February 2004.

Mike Kennedy, "Responding to Tragedy," *American School and University,* April 1, 2004.

John Lott, "The Missing Gun," *American Enterprise,* April/May 2002.

Paul J. McNulty, "Drugs, Guns and Violence," *Law & Order,* December 31, 2003.

Natalie Pompilio, "Every Day of the Year, Somebody's Getting Killed," *Philadelphia Inquirer,* May 2, 2006.

Jeff Snyder, "Violence and Nonviolence: Part 1," *American Handgunner,* September 1, 2005.

———, "Violence and Nonviolence: Part 2," *American Handgunner,* March 1, 2006.

———, "Violence and Nonviolence: Part 3," *American Handgunner,* May 1, 2006.

Star-Ledger (Newark, NJ), "A Law Full of Holes," March 19, 2006.

INDEX

PICTURE CREDITS

Cover: Getty Images
AP Photo/Douglas Healey, 96
AP Photo/Las Vegas Sun, R. Marsh
  Starks, 78
© Carlos Avila Gonzalez/San
  Francisco Chronicle/CORBIS,
  32
Getty Images, 23, 26, 42, 83, 84
© Gideon Mendel/CORBIS, 58
© Les Stone/Sygma/CORBIS, 31
MAI/Landov, 7
Matthew Fearn/EMPICS /Landov,
  87

Maury Aaseng, 12, 19, 37, 52, 62,
  72, 91
© Peter Johnson/CORBIS, 8
© Philip Wallick/CORBIS, 38
© Reuters/CORBIS, 20, 95
Reuters/Fabrizio Bensch /Landov, 46
Reuters/Keith Bedford /Landov, 50
Riccardo De Luca/Maxppp
  /Landov, 49
© Scott Houston/Sygma/CORBIS,
  68
Stone/Getty Images, 57
Time Life Pictures/Getty Images, 71

ABOUT THE EDITOR

Ronnie D. Lankford Jr. lives in Appomattox, Virginia, with his wife, seven cats, and a rat. Schirmer Trade published his first book, *Folk Music USA: The Changing Voice of Protest*, in 2005. This is is first publication with Greenhaven Press.

WITHDRAWN

No longer the property of the
Boston Public Library.
Sale of this material benefits the Library.